For those of us who have often suffered the inevitable humiliating regression back to childhood during every holiday with the family ... this book offers real help to the reader to develop the self-protective art of indifference, a cloak that can be used at many a holiday gathering ... and to understand the subtle yet profound differences between ineffective and effective confrontation, empathy and sympathy, and attaching response and defusing strategy ... a completely new cupboard of techniques.

—Joel C. Frost, Ed.D., assistant clinical professor of psychology in the Department of Psychology at Harvard Medical School

Children of the Self-Absorbed *offers practical advice and guidance. The creative techniques and exercises are priceless to both the reader learning how to identify destructive parental behaviors and how to cope with them as well as the reader learning to nurture and protect his or her own developing self.*

—Saul Hopper, Ph.D., clinical psychologist in private practice in St. Louis, MO

Children of narcissistic parents are provided techniques to dig themselves out of impossible relationships with their parents ... a thoroughly well thought out, useful manual to help adult children move toward more productive connection to their narcissistic parents, to themselves, and to others.

—Joan Medway, Ph.D, LCSW, psychologist in private practice in Potomac, MD

Children
of the Self–
Absorbed

SECOND EDITION

A Grown-Up's Guide
to Getting Over
Narcissistic Parents

Nina W. Brown, Ed.D., LPC

New Harbinger Publications, Inc.

Publisher's Note

This publication is designed to provide accurate and authoritative information in regard to the subject matter covered. It is sold with the understanding that the publisher is not engaged in rendering psychological, financial, legal, or other professional services. If expert assistance or counseling is needed, the services of a competent professional should be sought.

Distributed in Canada by Raincoast Books

Copyright © 2008 by Nina W. Brown
New Harbinger Publications, Inc.
5674 Shattuck Avenue
Oakland, CA 94609
www.newharbinger.com

Acquired by Catharine Sutker; Cover design by BLUE DESIGN;
Edited by Carole Honeychurch; Text design by Tracy Carlson

Library of Congress Cataloging-in-Publication Data

Brown, Nina W.
   Children of the self-absorbed : a grown-up's guide to getting over narcissistic parents /
Nina W. Brown. -- 2nd ed.
       p. cm.
   Includes bibliographical references (p.   ).
   ISBN-13: 978-1-57224-561-7 (pbk. : alk. paper)
   ISBN-10: 1-57224-561-1 (pbk. : alk. paper) 1. Parent and adult child. 2. Adult chil-
dren--Psychology. 3. Narcissism. 4. Family--Psychological aspects. I. Title.
HQ755.86.B76 2008
158.2'4--dc22

                                    2008002242

14 13 12

15 14 13 12 11 10 9 8

This book is dedicated to my children, Toni, Mike, and Linda, and to my grandchildren, Billy, Joey, Samantha, Chris, Nick, and Emma.

Contents

Acknowledgments

Many thanks are due to the readers of the first edition of *Children of the Self-Absorbed* who took the time and effort to write to me about their reactions and appreciation for putting complex concepts and feelings into words. Their feedback was very encouraging and heartwarming. The second edition could not have been conceived without their input.

Thanks are also due Catharine Sutker, who worked with me as the acquisitions editor for this book. It is due to her efforts that the manuscript was accepted, and I appreciate her efforts on my behalf. Carole Honeychurch, the copy editor, and Heather Mitchener, the editorial director, were instrumental in getting the manuscript ready for publication, and their efforts are greatly appreciated.

I want to acknowledge the support received from family and friends who are not in this field but who encouraged me nevertheless. Finally, I want to thank all who by their actions supplied me with material for the book.

Much happiness and good luck
Nina W. Brown
June 2007

Preface

The first edition of this book, *Children of the Self-Absorbed: A Grown-Up's Guide to Getting Over Narcissistic Parents* (2001), was written after a suggestion by an editor at New Harbinger, the book's publisher. I am very appreciative of the readers and therapists who were gracious and kind enough to write me about their reactions and experiences after reading that book. They let me know that the material was very helpful in understanding some long-term issues that were negatively impacting their self-perceptions, lives, and relationships.

That edition was able to put into words what some people experienced with their parent and helped explain many of their reactions to the behaviors and attitudes of the parent. I offered a title ("the Destructive Narcissistic Pattern") for a collection of hard-to-explain behaviors and attitudes and the impact of these. Also provided were information and strategies to help reduce feelings of being alone in this experience and to increase feelings of being understood by someone. That book did not take the place of work with a mental health professional, as that can be the best process for resolving deep-seated long-term issues and concerns and for building a new and stronger self.

The letters, phone calls, and e-mails I received were the impetus for the new edition. Questions readers asked pointed out some areas that could be expanded to be more helpful or where more information and explanations were needed, and asked for specific suggestions for certain situations, such as coping with the aging self-absorbed parent. These inquiries and suggestions are the basis for the material in this second edition.

Some 95 percent of the material in this second edition is new. This book addresses commonly occurring situations, such as celebrations, grandparent actions, and the aging parent, and I provide specific ways to identify the lingering, hidden, and toxic effects on you of parental self-absorption. Much of this book is given to providing specific strategies to reduce negative parental effects, strengthen your self, and build a new and better self.

HOW TO USE THIS BOOK

The intended procedure for reading this book is that each chapter be read in order, and that the chapter exercises be completed before proceeding to the next chapter. Each chapter builds on the material and personal learning from the preceding one to provide progressive understanding. Further, you may want to gather the following materials in advance so that exercises can be completed promptly without having to search for or buy materials. Materials that are generally used include sheets of plain paper, index cards, pens or pencils for writing, and a set of crayons, felt marker pens, or colored pencils for drawing.

Finally, you will see that I alternate use of gender specific-pronouns in the chapters to make the discussion easier to read. Both genders are always meant; for example, when the word "she" is used, both he and she are meant. Chapters 1, 3, 5, 7, and 9 use she and her, and chapters 2, 4, 6, 8, and 10 use he and him.

THERE IS HOPE

Though the issues and emotions connected to your self-absorbed parent may seem intractable at times, take heart: You do not have to stay mired in misery. You can take steps that will enable you to better cope with the distressing behaviors and attitudes of your self-absorbed parent and begin the delayed process of growth and development that may not have occurred for you because of this parent.

CHAPTER 1

Infuriating, Critical, Demanding, and Unreasonable Parents

Below, is a composite message I derived from the ones received from readers of the first edition of this book. These statements, addressed to the self-absorbed parent, capture many of the feelings that grown-up children of these parents experience. Some address their mothers, and some their fathers. See if any of their words resonate with your experience or feelings.

It's all about you, and you make sure of that. Your wants, needs, and demands are always the main focus. Everything must be done your way, or it's not acceptable. You never stop to consider that others have rights too. In your eyes, you know what is best and are always right, and I have to fall in line or incur your wrath, displeasure, and disappointment.

You are completely self-serving. You use every situation to fulfill your needs. You are blind to others' needs, deaf to their emotions, and expert at manipulation. You work hard to trigger my guilt, sadness, rage, and shame, and to make sure that I am exactly what you want me to be. You constantly berate, blame, and criticize me, and I am always miserable around you.

I want to please you, but I never seem to be able to. You are like a hurricane. I know you are coming so I prepare for the damage you can do, but my preparations are in vain. After you leave, I am left with the residual emotions to clean up, while you move on not knowing or caring about the destruction you cause to me or to anyone else.

How I long for some sign that you like and love me, but in all my years with you, I've never felt this, and this lack affects me deeply. As I was growing up, you never showed any understanding of what I was feeling, and when I tried to make you understand, you either ignored or minimized my feelings or became angry and said that I was ungrateful or disrespectful for criticizing you.

Now that I am an adult, I find that I still long for your love. I know that you cannot be different, but that doesn't take away the yearning for a more satisfying and loving relationship.

What most readers have in common is an awareness that their childhood experiences are continuing to exert unwanted and negative effects on them as adults, and that they want to do something to moderate or eliminate these. The first edition of *Children of the Self-Absorbed* described the actions and attitudes of destructive narcissistic parents that had enduring and deep negative effects on their children. This group of actions and attitudes was characterized as a Destructive Narcissistic Pattern (DNP). Some effects were obvious to the children as they grew older but still exerted their corrosive effects on the children's self-esteem, self-confidence, and self-efficacy. As well as describing the problem, I offered guidelines and suggestions to help grown children cope with these negative effects and to build and fortify their adult selves to help prevent further injury and corrosion. In this second edition, I extend that material and offer strategies that can help you to:

- Manage and contain the difficult feelings aroused in interactions with the self-absorbed parent

- Prevent self-defeating thoughts and change self-defeating attitudes

- Implement specific actions to ease difficult situations, such as holiday gatherings, events that produce rage, and even interactions between your parent and your children

- Recognize the lasting negative effects of parental destructive narcissism and how to overcome or moderate these

- Handle blame and critical or demeaning comments from anyone, including your parent

- Construct your self, your life, and your relationships to be meaningful and satisfying

- Modify the old, negative parental messages that still affect your behavior and emotions

- Get over some deep injuries from the parent

- Recognize your own undeveloped narcissism and take steps that could promote growth and development of healthy adult narcissism

As you read and work through the exercises provided, you can expect to have some difficult memories triggered, to have repressed and suppressed long-standing issues and concerns emerge into awareness, and to recognize unfinished business. Although you probably don't relish the idea of having these thoughts and feeling these emotions, doing so is a necessary first step in understanding your experience and beginning the process of change. Change can be difficult, but this book suggests specific actions and offers guidance for moderating or eliminating the negative effects of the parental DNP. You don't have to continue to suffer and be frustrated. There are ways that you can help yourself. As you read, you will gain understanding about and strategies to help improve:

- Interactions with the parent and triggered negative feelings

- Thoughts about your self and other basic attitudes

- Relationships with the parent and with others

- Your ability to manage difficult events and situations

I encourage you to use the scales and exercises in this book to gain greater awareness and understanding, and to adopt those suggested strategies that best fit your personality.

NARCISSISM DEFINED

The term "narcissism" has been used quite a bit so far. *Narcissism* can be defined as the adult's self-love, self-esteem, and feelings about her essential self. On one end, there is healthy adult narcissism that is mature and realistic (Kohut 1977). On the other end, there is pathological narcissism that is extremely immature, unrealistic, and completely self-serving. In between the two ends lies undeveloped narcissism, where some aspects of the person have progressed to the healthy end, some may still be in the immature range, and still others are in the process of developing. Think of the immature range as that which contains behaviors and attitudes expected of infants and children but signals immaturity and undeveloped narcissism in adults, such as constantly boasting or bragging, expecting others to immediately meet their demands without protest, or taking unnecessary risks that can be very self-destructive.

This definition of narcissism is not evaluative or judgmental—it is simply descriptive of a collection of behaviors and attitudes that reveal how someone perceives and feels about her self, the degree of perceived separateness and individuation from others, and how she perceives and feels about others. We will focus on these revealing behaviors and attitudes and begin to understand their impact on relationships, how their growth and development are lacking and how this growth can be facilitated, and how this lack of growth and development is unconscious and not known to that person. It is the last point that can present difficulties for others in a relationship, as the person with immature or undeveloped narcissism is unaware that she exhibits behaviors and attitudes reflective of an earlier stage of development and tends to be oblivious of the impact these have on others.

The information and strategies you will find in this book can be of enormous help to you in your interactions with your parent and in your everyday life. But no book can take the place of working with a competent mental health professional who can guide your personal development. That work can produce the deep understanding and personal changes you may desire, and I encourage you to seek out this expertise and guidance. This book will be an excellent starting point and ally in your journey, but nothing can fully substitute for professional help.

THE SELF-ABSORBED PARENT

Self-absorption occurs when there is a continual and extreme focus on one's self in almost every situation and circumstance. Actions by self-absorbed people are based on their needs most or all of the time, even when some acts seem to benefit others. This book presents this continual and extreme self-focus as a Destructive Narcissistic Pattern (Brown 1998, 2001, 2006).

Following are the behaviors and attitudes that are descriptive of a DNP. Read the descriptions through first, and then complete the rating scale that follows.

- **Grandiosity:** The person tends to see herself as a sort of superwoman, with unreasonable expectations for her success, performance, wealth, and the like. She feels she must win all of the time and that she knows what's best for others.

- **Entitlement attitude:** This attitude is one that assumes that everyone is just an extension of her self and therefore others are under her control and just exist to meet her needs, even unspoken ones. Others are not recognized as separate and distinct individuals. She expects and demands preferential treatment and feels that her needs should receive priority over the needs of others.

- **Lack of empathy:** She is indifferent to the impact of her critical, demeaning, and devaluing comments and remarks but simultaneously expects others to be empathic to her. She constantly blames others for mistakes and what cannot be changed.

- **Extensions of self:** Since the person does not recognize others as separate from her, she expects favors but does not return them. She gives orders and expects these to be promptly carried out, and expects others to read her mind and know what she wants without having to speak. She asks intrusive personal questions and tells others what they should or ought to do, but she doesn't respect others' property or boundaries.

- **Impoverished self:** The behaviors that signal the impoverished self includes constantly decrying how she is deprived, left out, and minimized, even when there is no evidence to support this perspective. She can be self-depreciating but will become angry or hurt if others agree. She uses put-downs of herself in an effort to get others to disagree.

- **Attention seeking:** Most of these behaviors and attitudes are easily seen as the person usually or always does some or all of them. She not only speaks loudly, she talks a lot. She enters and exits rooms noisily, dresses to attract attention, and makes grand gestures.

- **Admiration seeking:** These behaviors are those that are constantly done for public approval and approbation, which the parent craves as external signs of worthiness, superiority, and the like. She boasts and brags about accomplishments and promotes herself for awards and other recognitions. She responds to flattery but does not recognize insincere compliments.

■ **Shallow emotions:** This person expresses and experiences few emotions, usually only anger and fear. She has the words for feelings, but these are empty.

■ **Envious:** This person displays envy when she says and does things that reflect resentment of others' success, accomplishments, possessions, or opportunities, and feels that she is more deserving. Feelings of envy can trigger the impoverished self.

■ **Contemptuous:** Contempt is a part of feeling superior, where the person thinks that others are less deserving, worthwhile, or valuable. She will make negative and demeaning comments about others' value and worth, such as poor people not deserving assistance.

■ **Arrogant:** This attitude of feeling vastly superior to others can be seen in behaviors such as talking down or patronizingly to others. She is not shy about letting others know that she perceives them as inferior and makes frequent references to her superiority.

■ **Empty at the core of self:** The empty person perceives relationships as existing for her convenience and hops from relationship to relationship, never able to make real connections. She is unable to form and maintain meaningful, satisfying, and enduring relationships, becomes very anxious when alone, and seems to crave or need activity. _Supply_

■ **Reverses parenting and nurturing:** The child is made responsible for the parent's well-being instead of the usual reverse expectation. Behaviors that signal this attitude include statements like the following: "If you loved me, you would…"; "I love you when you…"; "Don't you want me to love you?"; "You make me feel good when you…"; "I don't like it when you disappoint me"; "Can't you ever do what I want or need you to do?"

- **Basks in the child's reflected glory:** This parent demands that the child become and do what she desires, for example, by excelling in athletics and school achievement or displaying other talents. The child must be very successful or the parent will be displeased. She is indifferent to or ignores the child's desires.

- **Intolerant of child's values, needs, and so on:** She cannot perceive the child as a separate and distinct individual but only as an extension of her. She cannot tolerate disagreement or any hint of criticism, as she should always be perceived as perfect, and blames the child for perceived imperfections and mistakes.

- **Exploits others:** This behavior and attitude are also reflections of an inability to perceive and relate to others as separate, different, and worthwhile individuals. Others are perceived as existing for her benefit and subject to exploitive behaviors, such as taking unfair advantage of others, manipulating others to get her own way, and assuming unearned credit.

Assess your parent on the items below using the following ratings and the previous definitions.

The Parental DNP Scale

5—Very much like your parent; always or almost always

4—Often like your parent; very frequently

3—Sometimes like your parent; many times

2—Occasionally like your parent; infrequently

1—Not at all like your parent; never or almost never

1. Grandiosity   5 4 3 2 1

2. Entitlement attitude   5 4 3 2 1

3. Lack of empathy   5 4 3 2 1

4. Extensions of self   5 4 3 2 1

5. Impoverished self   5 4 3 2 1

6. Attention seeking   5 4 3 2 1

7. Admiration seeking   5 4 3 2 1

8. Shallow emotions   5 4 3 2 1

9. Envious   5 4 3 2 1

10. Contemptuous   5 4 3 2 1

11. Arrogant   5 4 3 2 1

12. Empty at the core   5 4 3 2 1

13. Reverses parenting and nurturing   5 4 3 2 1

14. Basks in the child's reflected glory   5 4 3 2 1

15. Intolerant of child's values, needs, and the like   5 4 3 2 1

16. Exploits others   5 4 3 2 1

Scoring: Add your ratings to obtain a total score. Use the following as a guide to understanding the ratings.

65–80: The parent has considerable behaviors and attitudes reflective of a DNP.

49–64: The parent has numerous behaviors and attitudes reflective of a DNP.

33–48: The parent has some behaviors and attitudes reflective of a DNP.

17–32: The parent has a few of the behaviors and attitudes reflective of a DNP.

0–16: The parent has almost none, or none, of the behaviors and attitudes reflective of a DNP.

What you probably realized from completing this scale is that your parent had some characteristics but not others, or at least she had lower ratings on some items. But if your ratings for your parent totaled 49 or more, then you perceive her as having numerous characteristics reflective of self-absorption. Later in this chapter, you will find descriptions for various types of self-absorbed parents, and your parent's behavior and attitudes can be reflected in a particular type. But it's important to remember that these descriptions and categories are not definitive. They are used for ease of discussion.

THE CHILD WHO ASSUMED PARENT RESPONSIBILITIES

The self-absorbed parents described here have many of the characteristics described in the scale and, in addition, have a conscious or unconscious expectation that their children are responsible for their, the parents', welfare instead of the reverse. Children growing up under these circumstances experience all or most of the following. These children:

- Exist as extensions of the parent

- Remain under parental control even as the children become adults

- Must meet parental expectations at all times, even as adults with their own needs and self-expectations

- Should be able to anticipate parental needs and desires and work diligently to fulfill these

- Must attend to and at all times admire the parent

- Are expected to sacrifice their lives and welfare to take care of the parent

- Should show empathy to the parent but not expect or receive empathy in return

- Must never make mistakes or show poor judgment, as this reflects negatively on the parent

- Are expected to drop what they are doing at any moment if the parent wants them to

- Should never exercise any independence or autonomy

The children of the self-absorbed, who experience these behaviors and attitudes from birth, are not allowed to become separate and distinct individuals in their own right and may find that this affects their adult lives in often negative ways.

To determine if this description fits you, read the following list of thoughts, feelings, and attitudes, and assess yourself on each using the following ratings.

Enduring Effects of the Parental DNP Scale

5—Always or almost always

4—Very often

3—Frequently

2—Seldom

1—Never or almost never

1. Difficulty forming satisfying and meaningful
   relationships that endure   5 4 3 2 1

2. Inability to recognize when others are trying
   to manipulate you to do things that are not in
   your best interests   5 4 3 2 1

3. Find it difficult to express a wide variety
   of emotions   5 4 3 2 1

4. Become overwhelmed by others' emotions and
   find it hard to let go of these   5 4 3 2 1

5. Become enmeshed in others' emotions   5 4 3 2 1

6. Tend to take comments and actions personally   5 4 3 2 1

7. Have difficulty controlling negative feelings,
   such as anger and resentment, and are bothered
   by these   5 4 3 2 1

8. Stay on edge and anxious about trying to
   please others   5 4 3 2 1

9. Have difficulty making decisions   5 4 3 2 1

10. Wonder why others seem to find more
    happiness and pleasure than you do   5 4 3 2 1

Add all your ratings to derive a total score.

The higher scores indicate more enduring negative effects that may have their roots in having grown up with a destructive narcissistic parent. Use the following as a guide to understand your scores.

41–50: Your behavior and attitudes indicate intense and enduring negative effects.

31–40: Your behavior and attitudes indicate considerable enduring negative effects.

21–30: Your behavior and attitudes indicate moderate negative effects.

11–20: Your behavior and attitudes indicate some negative effects.

0–10: Your behavior and attitudes indicate few or no negative effects.

Higher scores (35 or more) can indicate that you are still affected by old parental messages that direct your thinking and actions in ways that aren't always in your best interest. For example, if you rated item number 2 at a 4 or 5, you are too often manipulated into doing things you don't want to do, and there are probably times when your parent continues to do this to you, even though you are an adult. Examine each item and decide if your thoughts and actions are in your best interest most of the time. In your current relationships, are you reacting to others in terms of how you were expected to relate to your parent?

Effects of Reverse Parenting

One of the most troubling and enduring effects of reverse parenting can be a heightened emotional susceptibility. Emotional susceptibility is the tendency to "catch" others' feelings (usually negative feelings), incorporate these feelings into your self, and then find that you are unable to easily release them. Your psychological boundary strength was not sufficiently developed as you were growing up, so you're less able to screen out and choose which emotions of others you can accept and which the other person should keep. Do you find that you do any or all of the following?

- Constantly monitor others and try to discern what they are feeling

- Become upset when others are in distress

- Feel that you must have others' liking and approval most all of the time

- Take on the responsibility for others' welfare and/ or emotional well-being, even if they are independent adults who can care for themselves

- Remain on the alert for signs that others are in distress or are uncomfortable

- Stay on edge, churned up, or even upset and cannot let go of these feelings

- Feel fearful of any signals that there is conflict present, even when you are not involved

- Feel positive or happy only when those around you are feeling the same way

If you identify with these states, beliefs, and/or feelings, you may have sufficient emotional susceptibility so that you frequently experience what is called *projective identification*—that is, you catch, incorporate, and act on others' feelings that they project, and/or tend to become enmeshed or overwhelmed by others' feelings. You have trouble maintaining strong and resilient boundaries, where you can empathize without losing your separate identity and are able to let go of these feelings so that they do not endure.

To get some sense of the extent to which you experience emotional susceptibility, complete the following scale.

Enduring Effects of Reverse Parenting Scale

Assess the extent to which you have the experiences below using the following ratings.

5—Always or almost always; extremely

4—Frequently; very much

3—Sometimes

2—Seldom

1—Never or almost never

1. Find that you are doing something someone persuades you to do that you feel is imprudent or wrong   5 4 3 2 1

2. Are unclear about how you got into an uncomfortable situation   5 4 3 2 1

3. Try to please someone by doing something
   you don't want to do   5 4 3 2 1

4. Feel ashamed that you trusted someone
   who betrayed you   5 4 3 2 1

5. Find out that someone you value and respect
   does not value or respect you in return   5 4 3 2 1

6. Experience a sudden intensification of your
   feelings in an interaction   5 4 3 2 1

7. Feel guilty or ashamed when you are accused
   of being selfish or self-centered, especially
   by your parent   5 4 3 2 1

8. Get bullied into doing something to prove that
   you care for someone   5 4 3 2 1

9. Become sad when you sympathize with someone
   and are unable to let go of the sadness   5 4 3 2 1

10. Work hard to ensure harmony and smooth
    out any conflicts   5 4 3 2 1

Scoring: Add your ratings to achieve a total score.

41–50: You have considerable emotional susceptibility that may be a result of trying to please your self-absorbed parent but not succeeding.

31–40: You have a great deal of emotional susceptibility.

21–30: You have emotional susceptibility in many situations.

11–20: You have some emotional susceptibility.

0–10: You have little or no emotional susceptibility.

Let's examine some implications and impacts for each item.

IMPRUDENT AND WRONG

Some people are good persuaders and are able to convince others to do things that they may regret later. These people are usually strong emotional senders, and if your boundaries are not strong enough and/or you have a strong desire to please others, then you can get caught up in what they are sending. Then you can find yourself acting on what you've caught, even though a part of you is extremely reluctant. If you experienced reverse parenting, then you probably had many situations in which your parent was able to persuade you to do things you didn't want to do. Not that these were necessarily wrong or imprudent, but the pattern was set at that time, and you continue to act on it today.

UNCOMFORTABLE SITUATIONS

Do you frequently find yourself in uncomfortable situations and have little or no awareness of how you ended up there? You may be so susceptible to others' emotions that they are able to drag you along with them to carry their uncomfortable emotions so that they don't have to feel them. Reverse parenting experiences, such as a parent telling a child to come and make her feel better or claiming that what the child does and says "makes" her feel a certain way, can set the child up to assume and carry others' feelings. As an adult, the child can be hypersensitive to others' feelings, becoming enmeshed or overwhelmed by these and finding it hard to let go of them. These adult children often spend much of their time catering to others to ensure their emotional comfort so as to not catch others' uncomfortable or distressing feelings. Children can be very open to accepting others' feelings, particularly those of their parents.

PLEASING OTHERS

There can be numerous occasions where you do something you do not want to do just to please someone because you deeply care for that person, and what is being done does not violate your values, morals, ethics, or principles. Examples could be agreeing to a child's request to play when all you want to do is to take a nap, or helping when a friend needs a favor. However, if you find that you have a deep and enduring need to please others and this means that you are being manipulated and exploited, then you may be acting on an effect of reverse parenting where you were always expected to please the parent at your expense.

BETRAYED AND ASHAMED

There can be an awful feeling of rejection and abandonment when you are betrayed by someone you trust. Some people who had a reverse-parenting experience can feel that they are to blame—they weren't good enough to prevent the person from acting as she did or that they were inadequate in not being able to anticipate the betrayal. These people assume self-blame instead of blaming the betrayer. This lowered self-confidence, self-esteem, and self-efficacy can arise from childhood experiences where the child could not "get it right" or be sufficient for the parent's needs.

NOT VALUED AND RESPECTED

Finding out that someone you value and respect does not recipro-cate can produce the same feelings as when you are betrayed. Shame and guilt for not being good enough, humiliation for not immediately perceiving that the person did not value or respect you, and anger for the perceived unfairness are some common feelings. You may still be trying to get your self-absorbed parent's approval and liking at the expense of your feeling valued and respected. Hence, you find it dif-ficult or impossible to immediately see when others don't value and respect you.

INCREASED AND INTENSIFIED FEELINGS

Intensified feelings in interactions are a strong signal of just how much you may be subject to projective identification experiences, where you unconsciously catch feelings during an interactions, incor-porate these on top of what you were already feeling (which increases and intensifies your existing feelings), and then act on the increased and intensified feelings. Further, you are usually unable to moderate these or to easily let go of them. You may even wonder why you are feeling as intensely as you do. Your psychological boundary strength is insufficient to prevent this projective identification.

ACCUSATIONS OF SELF-CENTEREDNESS AND SELFISHNESS

Accusations of self-centeredness and selfishness may or may not have some validity, but that's not the focus here. The focus is on your feelings about the accusation. When you immediately feel guilt and shame when charged with being self-centered or selfish, you usually cannot think clearly enough to adequately assess the accusation's validity. The result is that you either jump to act differently so as to negate the accusation, deny it, or become angry and turn it back on the accuser. Your reactions could be just what the other person desired, allowing her to further manipulate you, or so that the accuser can be shown as superior. This situation could be similar to what you experienced during your childhood reverse-parenting experiences.

BULLIED

Bullying can be physical, emotional, and/or psychological. The receiver can feel inadequate and helpless to prevent or stop the attacks. She can react in several ways, complying with the intimidating demands, feeling inferior to the bully, or agreeing for reasons unknown to her—acting like someone whose early experiences predispose her to perceive bullying as a way of showing caring or of getting attention. When she acts this way, she is reacting to the new situation in terms of old situations, but she is unaware of the connection. Physical bullying is usually very visible, and there are steps that can be used to relieve the situation, such as flight. Emotional and psychological bullying are harder and more complex to combat, and the reaction to bullying usually has its roots in family-of-origin experiences. Your reverse-parenting experiences may be a factor in your actions to do something you do not want to do just to please another person, much as you did with your parent. Your desire to please was more important to you than was maintaining your sense of integrity, or you felt powerless and fearful of abandonment. Either way, that pattern is continuing to get played out in your relationships today.

SAD

Any emotion could really be used to head up this section, as the major point is about your psychological boundary strength. If you cannot let go when you sympathize or experience intense feelings during an interaction, then you may not be experiencing only *your* feelings. It is likely that you have caught the other person's feeling, whatever that feeling was, and now are making it your feeling. Children have to develop healthy psychological boundary strength, and the reverse-parenting experience is unlikely to allow this to happen.

NEED TO ENSURE HARMONY

When you are emotionally susceptible—and everyone can be to some extent, particularly when you are with someone you care for—you work to ensure harmony because other people's distress arouses your distress, and you don't want to feel that way. You are really seeking harmony so as to take care of your feelings. You may also have assumed the same role in your family of origin and done so for the same reasons; that is, so that you did not have to take on the uncomfortable and distressing feelings engendered by the conflict. As an adult, you continue to feel that it is your responsibility to take care of everyone so that conflict does not emerge.

TWO RESPONSES TO A PARENTAL DNP

There are two major responses children seem to have when their parent has a DNP: compliant or rebellious. The compliant response has the child trying harder and harder to please the parent, a reaction that extends into adulthood, where anxiety is experienced when others do not seem to be pleased, and considerable effort goes into trying to always please others. This response also includes searching anxiously for nonverbal signals of distress, desires, or needs; the inability to be content with less that perfection; never feeling adequate; and relying mostly on others for validation.

The rebellious response occurs when the child does not try to please the parent because she realizes that pleasing the parent is not possible. The child then acts in a way that conveys that she doesn't care what others think about her, does not try to discern what others want or need, keeps a distance from others, and retreats into a self-validation stance. This stance makes it difficult for this person to trust others and works against establishing meaningful and satisfying relationships.

IS YOUR PARENT A DESTRUCTIVE NARCISSIST?

Before we explore further the possibility that you may have grown up with a parent with a DNP, let's do an exercise that will help you describe your parent more fully.

Exercise 1.1: Description of Your Parent

Materials: One or more sheets of paper and a pen or pencil for writing, and a suitable writing surface.

Procedure: Sit in silence and let your thoughts focus on your parent. Try to contain and manage the feelings aroused in you for the present time.

1. Quickly, without evaluating or editing, write ten or more adjectives that describe the parent that you think may have a DNP.

2. Now, list the feelings aroused in you as you think about this parent.

3. Write a summary paragraph that describes your parent, using some or all of the adjectives and feelings.

4. Title your summary.

5. Put this description away in a safe place where you can refer to it at points throughout the book to see if your feelings have changed. Try reading this after each chapter.

Types of Self-Absorbed Parents

There are many self-absorbed behaviors and attitudes, and it can be confusing when your parent has some but not others. So, for ease of discussion, I will describe four types of self-absorbed parents. These are needy, prickly, conniving, and grandstanding. Each will be presented, with a basic description, a list of behaviors, and the possible responses of the compliant child and the rebellious child.

NEEDY

The needy self-absorbed parent can come across to others as very caring and concerned. This parent is usually attentive, tries to anticipate every need, and is very anxious about getting recognition for her efforts. This need for recognition, specifically, is very suggestive of self-absorption. This parent has to receive attention, appreciation, and approval for almost every parental act, both from the child and from others. The child is not cared for altruistically—the child is expected to "pay" for the care with emotional coin. Any suggestion that the parent's efforts are not wanted or appreciated, such as a toddler exerting her burgeoning independence, can result in the parent's displeasure or in her taking control and managing the child; for example, by overprotecting. This parent makes sure others know how hard she works, sacrifices, and cares, to the extent that no one can ever over-look or forget about it.

Behaviors and Attitudes

- Clingy

- Overly nurturing

- Overprotective

- Makes a big deal out of perceived personal sacrifices

- Complaining

- Gets anxious when alone

- Wants to know your every thought, feeling, and so on

- Feelings are easily hurt

- Never forgets an offense, such as a slight or a critical remark

- Never empathic but can seem very sympathetic

- Uses soothing behavior to keep you from experiencing your feelings

PRICKLY

The prickly self-absorbed parent is very demanding and expects prompt and accurate compliance with her needs, whether or not these needs were verbally conveyed. Others are expected to "do the right thing," to always "do it right," without ever having an adequate explanation for what "right" means for this parent. Deviations from the self-absorbed parent's internal understanding of "right" cannot be tolerated, and the child endures constant criticism and other negative comments. This parent can also be very touchy, sensing disapproval, criticism, and blame from almost everything that is said and done, whether or not that is what was meant. As a consequence, others can always be on edge around this parent, are careful in what they do and say, and continue to try to "get it right" or withdraw physically and/or emotionally.

Behaviors and Attitudes

- Critical and criticizing

- Never completely satisfied

- Picky—everything must be done to her perceptions and standards

- Demands perfection

- Hypersensitive to perceived criticism

- Blames others when she is uncomfortable, and also blames you when you are uncomfortable

- Makes demeaning or devaluing comments to and about others

- Takes offense easily

- Nags

CONNIVING

The conniving self-absorbed parent is always positioning herself to win, come out on top, be superior to others, and make sure that all others understand just how they are inferior. This applies to almost all aspects of her life, including her children. This parent will lie, cheat, distort, and mislead in order to achieve her goals. Others are considered fair game for manipulation and exploitation, including her children. She can be adept at reading other's needs and emotional susceptibility and using these to manipulate and exploit them. Some effects on these parents' children as adults are a wariness and constant questioning of others' motives or a tendency to get into relationships where they are manipulated to do things they do not want to do or that aren't in their best interests.

Behaviors and Attitudes

- Manipulative

- Has to win at all costs

- Lies, cheats, misleads, and distorts

- Coercive, seductive

- Ingratiating to get what is wanted

- Takes advantage of others

- Is dismissive of others as inferior

- Vengeful

- Assumes that others are supposed to do what she wants them to do

- Always looks for the main chance, an edge, and the like

GRANDSTANDING

The grandstanding parent can be described as "always on stage," "playing to the crowd," "larger than life," and other such descriptors. Others in her world have to assume a subordinate role, and that role must support and highlight this parent's self-perception. Her children are perceived as extensions of her and exist to enhance and expand the areas where the parent can be admired, receive attention, be better than others, and so on. The child must never fail; and when the child succeeds, that success is perceived as due to the parent's efforts or contributions. The effects on her children can produce someone who is timid, cautious, and always seeking attention and admiration, or someone who acts out to get the same outcomes.

Behaviors and Attitudes

- Flamboyant, dramatic

- Restless, moves from person to person, project to project, thought to thought

- Maniacal at times, talks fast, moves fast, and expects others to follow this lead

- Boasts and brags constantly

- Resents anyone who outshines her

- Exaggerates accomplishments and ailments

- Engages in considerable self-promotion

- Overestimates her abilities, capabilities, and talent

- Intrusive, ignores or fails to recognize others' psychological boundaries, possessions, or territory

- Assumes she is in charge

Effects of Types on the Child

Now we'll take a look at how each parental type affects the children involved, focusing particularly on the two major ways that children usually respond to these parents: compliance or rebellion.

NEEDY

- **Compliant response:** The compliant child who has a needy narcissistic parent can become overly sensitive to others' needs. She constantly monitors others for signs of distress, unmet needs, and the like. The child tries to read other people's minds, attempting to know how to behave even before a request is made. She is very anxious and fearful of disagreements and other forms of conflict. She subordinates personal needs most of the time, feels guilt and shame when others are disappointed, and does things that she doesn't want to do in trying to please others. Children of the needy parent can be easily seduced and often become enmeshed in others' feelings.

- **Rebellious response:** When the child responds rebelliously, the behavior of the needy narcissistic parent results in the child keeping others at a distance and often refusing to connect or engage. These children can be insensitive or can ignore others' needs. They tend to openly disagree with others but then withdraw from conflict. They are resentful when others try to seduce or coerce them.

PRICKLY

- **Compliant response:** Compliant children who have a prickly narcissistic parent try hard to please and can be fearful of conflict. A child in this situation tends to be a perfectionist but feels like an imposter when she actually achieves or is complimented. She cringes at the slightest hint of criticism or blame, can be bullied, and tries to discern what is expected and comply.

- **Rebellious response:** When the response to the prickly parent is rebellious, the child is defiant, tends to be combative, and is overly defensive in response to comments she perceives as critical. She tries to attack first as a defense, is not concerned with pleasing others, and does not recognize or accept support from others.

CONNIVING

- **Compliant response:** The compliant response to a conniving narcissistic parent will have a facade of the false self. The child will be overly complimentary and ingratiating but also sneaky and loose with the truth. She can be easily seduced or coerced, is fearful of being rejected, and is anxious and never confident about what to expect.

- **Rebellious response:** When the child's response to the conniving narcissistic parent is rebellious, she is wary of others, tending to mistrust their motives. She can be hard to get to know, as she is fearful of being coerced or seduced. She resents others trying to take advantage (or even the perception that this is happening) and is constantly on guard for others' hidden agendas.

GRANDSTANDING

- **Compliant response:** The compliant child of a grandstanding narcissistic parent will tend to be submissive, self-effacing, and self-deprecating. She is always on edge, trying to anticipate the unexpected and fearing and expecting the worst, and she is unable to protect her boundaries.

- **Rebellious response:** The rebellious child engages in risky behavior that can be self-destructive. She uses flattery as a tool and can appear cooperative but may have quiet or hidden defiance. She has considerable resistance to others' ideas, thoughts, and so on but is adept at concealing true feelings.

At this point, you have some indications of whether or not your parent has many of the behaviors and attitudes of the DNP and have identified your primary response as either compliant or rebellious. There can be some overlapping of categories, types, and responses, but the types are only provided for ease of discussion, and you can make adjustments to what is presented to fit you and your situation.

The material in the rest of this book is intended to guide you to a better understanding of how you developed and grew to become the person you are at this time, to teach you strategies that can be helpful when interacting with your self-absorbed parent, and to show you how to lessen or eliminate the negative impact of her behavior and attitudes on you. Among some gains you can experience are:

- Learning a process for containing and managing your difficult feelings

- Becoming more realistic about your parent and relinquishing the fantasy that the parent will change

- Discovering what to do and say in interactions with the parent—actions that can prevent your negative feelings from being aroused

- Building your capacity for empathy, creativity, and other characteristics of healthy adult narcissism

- Reducing your faulty beliefs and your undeveloped narcissism

- Overcoming many of the lingering effects on you produced by living with a parent with a DNP

- Learning strategies for how to handle difficult situations with the parent

- Gaining the freedom to become the person you want to be

CHAPTER 2

Lingering Effects of Parental Self-Absorption

There can be numerous lingering effects of your parent's self-absorption because your self was injured and was not allowed to be fully developed, and this is termed *narcissistic wounding*. You, of course, did not recognize what was happening at the time and may not yet be fully aware of how your childhood experiences continue to affect your adult self, your relationships, and your personal actions. Your parent's responses to you, his conscious and unconscious messages to you about your self, and your personality and responses to your parent all interacted to produce the injuries and lack of development you are probably dealing with today.

The parent's response to you as a developing child carried considerable importance for your self-esteem. Parental empathic attunement and responding helps build a child's self-esteem, and if your parent was unable or unwilling to provide sufficient empathy because of his self-absorption, then you did not receive the empathy that would be conducive to feeling worthy, cherished, and loved. While not all of your self-esteem is affected by empathy or its lack, you may still be struggling with major self-esteem deficits.

Parental conscious and unconscious messages are also received by the child consciously and unconsciously, incorporated into the self, and acted on, usually in nonconscious ways. That is, you are not aware of how these messages are affecting your thoughts and feelings about your self, your attitudes and responses to and about others, and your actions. These parental messages are powerful influences. You received messages about how your parent perceived your value as a person, your looks, your intelligence and abilities, your role in the family, expectations for what you were to be and do, how much you were loved, and other such messages. It's not hard to understand the importance and the continuing effects of parental messages.

Each person is different, and each has a unique personality and response to his parents. These interact and produce results unique to each person, although some can be generalized. That is, everyone with a self-absorbed parent has injuries to his self, but different people are injured in different ways. In this chapter, we'll be looking at some possible effects of incorporated parental messages on adult children of self-absorbed parents.

WERE YOU INJURED?

How can you begin to understand how you are narcissistically wounded, where you suffered an injury to your essential self that has not healed? The injury itself may have been forgotten, as it could have happened before you developed the capacity to store memories in the language you use and understand today (such as what can happen to infants and toddlers). These early injuries can still impact you in indirect, hidden, and masked ways. We are really talking about a belief that you must have intimate and close relationships in order to feel loved, competent, worthwhile, safe, and valued. While intimate and close relationships are enhancing and affirming, they should not be so compulsive that you will do things that are destructive or not in your best interest just to keep the relationship. What are some indicators that signal narcissistic wounding? Try the following exercise.

Exercise 2.1: Were You Injured?

Materials: Sheets of paper and a pen or pencil for writing

Procedure:

1. Sit in silence and think of a recent event or interaction that left you upset or feeling uncomfortable.

2. As you recall the event or interaction, assess your feelings (a through j) and their intensity using the following scale.

   5—This was an intense feeling for you at that time.

   4—This was a strong feeling.

   3—You felt this, but it was fleeting.

   2—You had a slight feeling like this.

   1—You did not feel this at all.

   a. You had a desire to retaliate or get even with the person.   5 4 3 2 1

   b. Your feelings were hurt.   5 4 3 2 1

   c. You felt embarrassed or humiliated.   5 4 3 2 1

   d. You became angry or enraged.   5 4 3 2 1

   e. You wanted to get away from the person and/or the situation.   5 4 3 2 1

   f. You wanted to attack or go on the offensive.   5 4 3 2 1

   g. You became sarcastic and used put-downs or other such responses.   5 4 3 2 1

   h. You felt inadequate or wrong.   5 4 3 2 1

   i. You thought about something else or changed the topic.   5 4 3 2 1

   j. You wanted to cry.   5 4 3 2 1

3. Select an item with a rating of 3 or higher. You will work with only one item at a time. As you start, you may want to select the one with the highest rating to work on. If this feels too raw or painful, select an item with a rating of 3. Once you have selected an item, sit back and close your eyes.

4. Explore the feelings around the selected item and try to identify all that you experienced. For example, if you selected "You had a desire to retaliate or get even with the person," reflect on what other feelings you were experiencing and when you wanted to retaliate or get even. You may have also experienced fear, shame, and disgust along with the anger. Become aware of all of the feelings, no matter how mild or fleeting they were. Open your eyes and make a list of these feelings.

5. Examine your list and identify the self-statement associated with each feeling. What were you thinking that triggered and increased the resulting emotion? For example, if you listed shame, the self-statement could be one or more of the following:

   ■ I am flawed, and others can see that.

   ■ I am not living up to my values and principles.

   ■ I was unable to protect myself.

   ■ I am not able to fix myself and be better.

   Examples for fear could include:

   ■ I am in danger of being seen as I really am and will be destroyed when this happens.

   ■ I cannot survive if others don't like me.

   ■ I will not get what I need to survive.

   ■ I cannot prevent others from destroying or abandoning me.

Write all self-statements on a sheet of paper.

6. Repeat steps 4 and 5 for each item rated 3 or higher. You may want to have a tally for each repeating statement. That is, if the self-statement appears for more than one item, don't write it again, just put a check by the first one each time it comes up again.

7. Note all the repeating self-statements and the most frequent and strongest emotions you experienced. How true do these statements feel as you read them? For example, if you answered that you are unable to protect yourself, how accurate is that self-statement? Give each an accuracy rating from 0 (completely inaccurate or false about you) to 10 (completely accurate or true). Note all self-statements that you rated as accurate at 5 or higher.

Beliefs About Your Self

Self-statements with an accuracy rating below 5 are some illogical and irrational thoughts you have that allow you to be wounded. These will be discussed in this chapter, and I will suggest substitute self-statements that are more reasonable and rational. The self-statements rated 5 or higher are either not under your control (for example, if you really *are* unable to protect yourself) or can be the goals for changes you can make (for example, learning and believing that you actually can survive if others don't like you).

You become injured because of your beliefs about your self, not because of what someone else says or does. If you did not have these beliefs about your self, then what others say or do would not produce these negative feelings. Some beliefs are conscious ones, and you are aware of them. Others are generally suppressed just below the level of awareness but can emerge at any time, while others are buried deep in your unconscious, and the only way you have any hint that they exist is through your reactions. You may consciously deny that you have these beliefs about yourself, but you would not have these negative feelings if you did not have some versions of these self-beliefs. Your challenge is to begin to know and understand your beliefs about yourself and to work to change those that are negative, defeating, and not constructive.

Self-statements that may be contributing to your injuries can include the following:

- I must have others' approval to survive.

- I have an obligation to be perfect.

- It is my responsibility to always take care of others.

- Others people's needs are more important than mine.

- I am flawed so badly that I cannot ever be better.

- I cannot survive without someone to take care of me.

- I must not let others see the real me, because they would then reject me.

- I am helpless to make changes or to take care of myself.

- I am not as good (able, intelligent, and so on) as others are.

- I can never get what I want or need.

Let's explore these for their validity, logic, and usefulness and develop some self-affirmations that can help counter the negative and illogical self-statements.

I REQUIRE OTHERS' APPROVAL

It feels supportive and encouraging when others approve of you. You can be confident that you are accepted and will not be abandoned or destroyed when you have their approval. While this may appear to be somewhat extreme as presented here, the fear that underlies the need for approval is very basic, even though it's usually not expressed as fear. Everyone has some fear of being abandoned or destroyed, and everyone wants approval.

If you received sufficient approval from family and other significant people in your early life environment, you developed enough self-confidence to believe that you are acceptable and will be supported and encouraged. If you have worked through some early life deficits, you've also developed this self-confidence. However, if your experiences were such that you received approval only for things like the following, then you may not think consciously or unconsciously that you receive sufficient approval:

- You always had to meet your parent's needs.

- You were expected to read your parent's mind and anticipate what he wanted or needed.

- Others told you they were pleased only for what you did for them and not for being who you are.

- You had major accomplishments that were a source of pride for the parent.

- You received parental approval only or mostly when you won and were successful.

Sufficient basic approval means that someone liked and accepted you as you were. That doesn't mean that you were always right or that he always approved of your behavior; it simply means that he could separate the two, you as a person from your behavior, and that his acceptance of you as a worthwhile and valued person did not waver, even when he was not pleased with your behavior or attitude. You could always count on him for support and encouragement.

If you did not receive this basic approval, or received it only for meeting other people's needs, then you may have developed a belief that you must meet others' needs, wants, and desires in order to count on their support for your survival. When you don't get their approval, or it appears that you don't have it, you can be wounded, as this tells you that you are not good enough. This is the message you received and internalized early on, and it continues to influence your behavior and beliefs about yourself. You work hard to gain and maintain others' approval and may even do things you do not want to do just to get their approval.

If this description is reflective of you some, most, or all of the time, you may want to explore this basic need of yours. You can use the following self-affirmation whenever you feel anxious that someone is not approving of you or that they may not approve of you.

SELF-AFFIRMATION: I like and want this person's approval, but I will be okay if I don't get it.

I MUST BE PERFECT

The belief that you have an obligation to be perfect can cause you much distress, as you can never be fully satisfied with your self. You never seem to quite reach perfection, and no external reassurance that you are good enough is sufficient to help you like or be more accepting of yourself. You may even extend your need to be perfect to others in your world and demand that they, too, be perfect. This extension to others can be detrimental to your relationships.

How did this belief come about? When did you internalize and make yours the conviction that the only way to survive was to be perfect? Notice that the belief is not to work for perfection—it is to *be* perfect. Even when you rationally know that perfection is not needed and cannot be attained, you cannot let go of your belief that you must be perfect. Your early experiences, such as the following, contributed to this belief:

- Parental criticism

- Lack of parental empathy for your errors and mistakes

- Blame for mistakes and errors, some of which was unfair

- Unrealistic parental expectations for your behavior

- Expressions of disappointment when your achievements, such as grades, were not perfect

- Unfair and unfavorable comparisons with siblings and others

- Receiving attention and admiration only when you met parental expectations

- Excessive parental expectations for neatness, cleanliness, and quiet behavior

It is difficult to pinpoint how or when you developed the belief that you have an obligation to be perfect, but knowing this may not be necessary for our purposes, which are to help you become more immune to narcissistic injury and to help you let go of old hurts and grudges.

What could be helpful is for you to realize that your focus on perfection is not constructive for you or for your relationships. You can act on this realization by working to become more satisfied with being good enough while still striving to be and do better. You can be perfect in some ways but still accepting of yourself and others as less than perfect in other ways. This will enable you to be less easily injured when you don't meet your expectations for perfection and when you don't meet others' expectations. You will be less shamed for not being perfect and more accepting of your flawed self as it is. Try the following self-affirmation whenever you start to be ashamed of what is less than perfect in your self. Practicing this can also lead you to become more accepting of the flaws in others.

SELF-AFFIRMATION: Being good enough is sufficient. I will work to be better, but I still like me.

I NEED TO TAKE CARE OF OTHERS

The key to this characteristic is the extent to which you think and feel that it is your responsibility to take care of others. It's reasonable for you to assume this responsibility for those who need this care, such as children or the elderly, or when such care is your job or profession, and it's perfectly okay to have care and concern for those who are less fortunate and in distress. What is not reasonable is for you to automatically assume responsibility for everyone, to be overly protective, to not accept and believe that others are capable of self-care, to be intrusive with your acts of caring, to insist that others accept these acts, or to feel guilty or ashamed when others are in distress. These are signs that you may be overly responsible, that you don't understand the limits of your personal responsibility and are unaware of others' desires for independence and autonomy. In these cases, you are most likely unconsciously trying to fulfill old parental messages. Thus, when you don't or cannot meet any or all of these demands on you, you become anxious, guilty, and/or ashamed.

It can be difficult to balance your expectations about taking care of others with the reality of the situation, their needs, and their self-care ability. This balancing act becomes even more difficult when you also tend to catch other people's feelings and have an unconscious need to act to reduce their feelings of distress so that you don't have to feel them too. The combination of feeling an obligation and catching feelings is a powerful one, and you will need to do much self-exploration to begin to understand why you are this way. That exploration is best done with the guidance of a competent mental health therapist.

How does feeling overly responsible for others' welfare contribute to your injury or reinjury? I've already presented one way—you feel guilty and ashamed, and that opens you up to feeling less positive about yourself. There are other situations that can produce guilt and shame, such as the following:

- A friend tells you to butt out of his business.

- Your help is rejected.

- You are chastised or blamed for not helping, or for failing to help, or for not helping enough.

- You are told that you are intrusive.

- Your child angrily tells you that he can handle his own affairs and doesn't need your help.

- You realize that your family is so dependent on you to do things for them that they are unable to care for themselves when you are sick.

- Your grown children expect you to do the same things you did for them in childhood.

- Your parent tells you or suggests that you are neglecting him.

- Your attempt to "fix it" are not appreciated.

You will want to keep the caring and helpful part of this and let go of the part that pushes you to always be the lead, front-and-center person and director of helpfulness. Learn when this is your responsibility and accept when it is not. Let others learn to take care of themselves, wait to be asked for your help, and encourage everyone, including your parents and children, to be as independent and self-sufficient as possible. Try the following self-affirmation before you rush to help.

SELF-AFFIRMATION: I may help more by showing confidence that the other person can fix it.

I MUST SEE TO OTHERS' NEEDS

Another belief that is closely associated with the previous one is a notion that others' needs are more important than yours are. There are times and circumstances where this is the case and you must subjugate your needs for those of someone else. For example, you may need to subjugate your needs if someone you love is ill, if you're caring for children or the elderly, and sometimes on the job. I'm not talking about situations such as these. I am talking about a mind-set that does not allow you to ever put your needs ahead of anyone else's.

Underlying your belief that others' needs are more important than yours are some thoughts and feelings similar to the following:

- It would be selfish for me to put my needs first.

- I must never, ever be perceived as selfish.

- I will not be liked, approved of, or supported if I am perceived as selfish.

- The way for me to get attention and admiration is to be self-sacrificing.

- I get taken advantage of because of my self-sacrifices.

- Others really appreciate what I am doing for them.

- I sometimes resent having to put others' needs before mine, but I would not feel right if I didn't do that.

- Even when I put others' needs first, I sometimes still feel guilty or ashamed that I didn't do enough or didn't do more.

You may have internalized early in your life that your needs were not as important as others' needs were. Lack of empathy from a parent or caretaker, neglect, blame, criticism, failure to accept you as you are and appreciate your qualities, and other such experiences could have shaped your belief that others' needs should be placed above your own. It will be difficult for you to overcome this and achieve a satisfactory balance between appropriate self-care and the need to take care of others. Whenever you're tempted or feel the need to take care of others before your needs get met, ask yourself, "Will the person or the relationship really suffer if I attend to my needs?" If the answer is that you would not feel right if you took care of your needs first, or that you would feel better if you put their needs first, then use the following self-affirmation.

SELF-AFFIRMATION: I deserve to be given preference sometimes, and self-care is also important.

I AM BADLY FLAWED

Despair, hopelessness, and helplessness are apt to emerge when you believe that you are so flawed that you can never get better. These feelings emerge at times when you are hurt and ashamed and can lead to depression. It can seem that no matter how hard you try, you continue to make the same mistakes and/or draw the same criticisms, blame, and other demeaning comments. You don't know why you can't "get it right" when other people don't seem to have that problem.

So, in addition to the hurt raised by external events, you can incur even more pain from your beliefs about your self. You may even feel, on some level, that you have many more flaws than do other people, although if someone were to ask if you thought this, you would probably deny it. You're hoping that others don't perceive you as you perceive yourself, although you really fear that they do.

You probably use a variety of attitudes, defenses, and other strategies to cover up your feelings and self-perceptions. Some examples of ways people cover up include the following:

- Arrogance (attitude)

- Superiority (attitude)

- Aggressiveness (defense)

- Rationalization (defense)

- Indifference (defense)

- Isolation and withdrawal (strategy)

■ Substance abuse (strategy)

You don't feel good about yourself, but you don't want others to know this because you fear that they would abandon or destroy you. This leaves you vulnerable to injury and reinjury, where the hurt self is subjected to even more pain. This happens many times over the years until it really doesn't take much at all to injure you.

Overcoming your negative self-perception and building a more positive one will take considerable time and effort, and I encourage you to get started right away. Some of the exercises in this book can help with your self-exploration, build your confidence in your self, and present alternative ways of perceiving, behaving, and relating. However, the real work may need the guidance of a competent therapist, and I encourage you to get this expert assistance. Until you've worked more, either alone or with assistance, try the following self-affirmation whenever you feel ashamed, hopeless, or helpless.

SELF-AFFIRMATION: I can do better and I will.

I NEED SOMEONE TO TAKE CARE OF ME

Usually, when someone thinks or feels that he needs another person to take care of him, the thought or feeling is about emotional and psychological caretaking. Adults who need physical care are correct in this belief and are not included in this discussion. We are really talking about needing intimate and close relationships with other people. Having such a belief about yourself can lead you to considerable hurt and feeling rejected. You can then be vulnerable to entering into destructive relationships, doing things you don't want to do, and tolerating acts that demean and devalue you. You will do almost anything to keep from being alone, but seem to derive little joy or satisfaction from your relationships. Even in a relationship, you feel alone.

Try the following exercise. If you become anxious or upset while doing it, immediately stop and focus on something that is pleasant or pleasing to you.

Exercise 2.2: Being Alone

Materials: Two sheets of paper and a pen or pencil for writing

Procedure:

1. Sit in silence, close your eyes, and visualize yourself as alone. Note your feelings, the images that emerge, any sounds or smells, and thoughts you may have.

2. When you are ready, open your eyes and write a description of the images that emerged. After you finish your description, write a list of feelings and other thoughts that emerged during the visualization.

3. Note the intensity of the negative feelings you experienced, and give them a rating from 0 (no intensity) to 10 (extremely intense).

4. Review the intensity ratings for step 3 and give each a validity rating. That is, rate how valid that feeling is when viewed realistically. Use ratings from 0 (not at all true) to 10 (very true).

5. Now write a sentence about each feeling you listed that captures the thought the feeling leads to. For example, if you felt fear, what did you fear?

6. Rate the validity of the resulting thought using 0 (not at all true) to 10 (very true).

7. Note how many feelings had thoughts with validity ratings of less than 5. Ratings of less than 5 could indicate that you may be needlessly worrying about things that are very unlikely to happen. Ask yourself if you can let go of these.

8. At a later date, repeat the exercise with a focus on the feelings with validity ratings of 5 or higher.

For the time being, try the following self-affirmation every day for the next month, or however long you wish.

SELF-AFFIRMATION: I am strong enough to survive on my own. I can build constructive and satisfying relationships.

I CAN'T REVEAL THE REAL ME

The real you may be hidden even from yourself. Everyone has aspects of self that they do not see but others do, and also aspects that are inaccessible for one reason or another. Uncovering our real selves can be a lifelong task. However, we are not attempting that major task here. We will be focusing on those aspects of yourself that you know about but want to keep hidden from others because you fear or expect that they will reject you if they should ever become aware of that part of you. You probably think of that part of your self as the "real" you. Thus, things others do or say that lead you to believe that they are aware of the real you can be painful as, in your mind, that awareness is most likely to lead to rejection.

Why do you feel that your real self must be hidden? There are many possible reasons, such as the following:

- Your real self was not responded to favorably early in your life, and you learned to display a false self.

- You grew up in a family where open expression of feeling was discouraged or even punished.

- When you expressed your thoughts and feelings, you were often told you were wrong or that you shouldn't feel that way.

- You didn't learn how to manage and contain your negative feelings.

- Your environment or culture did not encourage open and honest expressions of feelings.

- You are ashamed of some personal characteristics.

- You want others to perceive you in a positive and approving way, and you have some characteristics you think will preclude this acceptance.

- You have been badly hurt a number of times when you let some parts of your real self be revealed.

Whatever the reasons for hiding your real self, you can still be injured because you cannot fully hide everything you want to keep hidden. Yes, there are people who seem to be able to do this. But a careful examination of their situations and circumstances is likely to reveal that others did, in fact, see some of these supposedly shameful parts, but the wounded person refuses to consciously acknowledge that they were seen. They use denial, repression, and considerable rationalization to explain away what the other person saw or sensed.

You may want to explore for yourself the personal characteristics you want to keep hidden and why it is important to you to put on a facade. This doesn't mean that you need to reveal all your secrets or to be constantly telling others about characteristics that you perceive as less than desirable. You don't have to do either of these. It helps to simply be aware that you do have secrets and characteristics you prefer to keep hidden for fear that others will reject you.

SELF-AFFIRMATION: I can let more of my real self be revealed to others and, as I like parts of my self better, I can let more of my real self be seen by others.

I AM HELPLESS TO MAKE CHANGES

Have you tried to change something but were unsuccessful? If you're like most people, you have tried to change and became frustrated when there was no payoff, what you did was not entirely successful, or what you did seemed to make the situation worse. You may even have repeatedly tried to make changes, only to be unsuccessful.

This can be especially shaming when what you were trying to change was a personal characteristic, either one that you wanted to change or one that someone else wanted you to change.

Your lack of previous success could lead you to believe that you are helpless to change anything about yourself. You may believe that you can change some physical and external things, but that internal and psychological things are not under your control and that you are powerless. This belief can put you in a place where you start to feel helpless about other aspects of your life and your self, and can exacerbate low self-esteem, increase a lack of self-confidence, and reduce your self-efficacy. All these open you to becoming easily wounded, because you feel helpless to change at the same time you're being reminded that you are less than satisfactory and need to change.

What do you want to change about yourself, and why do you want these changes? What gets in the way of your being successful in making these changes? You are not helpless to make changes, although you may not have been successful in the past. You just haven't yet found what you need to do and how to do it. But, on some level, you may have convinced yourself that you are unable to do so because you are essentially flawed. This feeling of being flawed is what you find to be shaming and what continues to contribute to your feeling helpless.

Let's look at an example to illustrate this. Suppose you want to change your tendency to become easily angered. Your friends and family have told you on more than one occasion that you fly off the handle at the least little thing. You tried to change but were unsuccessful. You got suggestions from others about what to do, such as walking away from the situation. But when you tried them out, they did not seem to be helpful. You concluded that you were helpless to change because of a character flaw that "made" you need to vent.

A little self-exploration could reveal that you were easily angered when you experienced many or all of the following:

- Fear that others were trying to take advantage of you

- A belief that others thought you were stupid or not good enough

- A complete lack of control

- Guilt because you were not living up to others' expectations of you

- Fear of appearing weak and vulnerable

- Confusion about what to do or say

Rather than admit any of this to yourself, you externalized, projected, and displaced this on others and flew off the handle. You are ashamed of these thoughts and feelings, want to hide them, and don't know what to do to change them. Change involves several steps, beginning with understanding what you are experiencing. The next steps are to think through why you're reacting as you are, develop a plan for making changes one step at a time, and give yourself permission to not be entirely successful all at once. Some changes may need expert help, and that too can reduce your feeling of helplessness. A self-affirmation to try when you feel helpless about making personal changes may help.

SELF-AFFIRMATION: I can change, but I have not yet found a way to do it. I will not give up.

I'M NOT AS GOOD AS OTHERS

Other terms for thinking and feeling that you are not as good as others include low self-esteem, lack of self-confidence, and feelings of inferiority. All such terms and phrases point to a personal perception of one's self that is unfavorable when compared to other people. It also includes an unrealistic expectation that you are not worthy unless you are as good as or superior to others in every way. What's more realistic, and can lead to better self-acceptance, is the realization and acceptance that you have some strengths and some weaknesses. You have aspects of your self that need work or development—and others do too. You are not in a contest, there will not be winners and losers, and you are not helping yourself when you focus on these kinds of comparisons.

When you think and feel that you are not as good or as adequate as others, this leaves you open to injury and reinjury because you are constantly faced with evidence that other people are richer, smarter, more talented, better looking, of higher status, and so on. In addition, every mistake you make becomes more evidence for your negative belief about your self. Comments and remarks by others that appear to focus on your weaknesses and negative aspects can produce even more validations of your negative beliefs, and these are very wounding. Your self can remain in a constant state of hurt.

You may find it helpful to focus more on your strengths. Don't ignore or deny your weaknesses and what needs developing; continue to work on these. But try to get in the habit of not dwelling on them, as that can make them seem worse than they really are and does nothing that helps you overcome them. Overall, you are as worthwhile and valuable as other people, even with your flaws and faults. Try the following self-affirmation.

SELF-AFFIRMATION: Mistakes can be corrected. I will do better next time. I need to work on this, but that doesn't make me less worthwhile. I will make the most out of who I am, what I have, and what I am able to do.

I CAN'T GET WHAT I WANT OR NEED

If you think or feel that you can never get what you want or need, you have a belief that you lack self-efficacy. This belief may have been established early in your life, even as an infant, where there was a significant delay in attending in your needs, neglect, or even disinterest. An example might be a child in a family where one or more siblings were born close together. Competing needs for attention, and the parents feeling overwhelmed at times, could have meant that one child most often experienced a significant delay in getting his needs met. This state then produced the belief for that child that he could not (and would never) get his needs met, and this belief persisted into adulthood. No amount of evidence to the contrary seems to affect this deep and enduring belief.

Think about it. There are very few, if any, adults who cannot take care of most of their needs and wants, especially the basic needs. So, what this belief is proposing is that the person cannot get others to take care of him, not that his needs and wants are not being met. The finger of blame is pointed at someone else, as if another person should be responsible for meeting your wants and needs. This expectation is reasonable for infants, children, and incapacitated adults but is not reasonable for most functioning adults. You are responsible for meeting your needs and wants, not other people.

However, if you do have this belief, then when you are injured it can appear that someone is not willing to meet your needs and wants. You may even expect that another person, especially your romantic partner, will read your mind or intuitively anticipate your needs and wants and make sure they are met. You become disappointed and hurt when this fails to happen, and every failure reinforces your belief that your needs and wants will forever remain unfulfilled. Both you and your relationships suffer as a result.

What can be helpful for you is to have a clearer understanding of what wants and needs you have. Many people only have global and vague ideas about their wants and needs. For example, some people may say that they want and need love. This is a reasonable and universal need. However, love is not defined universally, and if you were to specify what you meant by the love you want and need, it would probably be different from others' definitions. Too, it could be that when your need for love is explored in depth, the actual longing is for the unconditional and total love the ideal parent gives to his child. It is not reasonable to expect another person to give an adult this unconditional and total type of love. Your unrealistic yearnings are helping to produce your hurt every time you have evidence that you don't have this kind of love. This same process of analysis could help you better understand what you want and need and have more realistic expectations of yourself and others.

SELF-AFFIRMATION: I can take care of getting most of my needs and wants met for myself.

HELPING YOURSELF

You now have some suggestions about how you may be opening yourself to injury. In other words, you don't have to hurt as much as you do, you don't have to let what others say and do become criticism and blame, your self can be secure and strong enough to be self-reflective but not shamed by everything, and you don't have to retain hurts, resentments, aggressive thoughts, and self-defeating beliefs. You can develop and fortify your self so that you have a greater sense of confidence, self-esteem, and self-efficacy. That development has begun if you have increased your awareness of some of your self-defeating behaviors and attitudes, and if you have tried some of the self-affirmations presented in this chapter.

There are some perceptual shifts you can make that will also help. This means that you change your current perception from one that may be self-defeating to another that is more constructive, logical, and realistic. You are not giving up the good parts of yourself when you make these perceptual shifts—you are helping these parts to be stronger and more helpful while at the same time reducing your shame, guilt, sense of inadequacy, fears, and other negative thoughts about yourself. Read each proposed perceptual shift carefully and reflect on your capacity to make the shift.

From	To
The need for others' approval	Self-approval
The need for perfection	Satisfaction with being good enough
Overly responsible	Reasonable and limited personal responsibility
Feeling inferior to others	Recognition and acceptance of personal strengths
Dependence	Independence, interdependence, and mutual caring
Lack of self-acceptance	Embracing all parts of your self, even parts you don't like and want to change
Helplessness, hopelessness	Doing what you can and letting go of the rest

CHAPTER 3

Still Hurting: The Child as an Adult

Injuries to the self inflicted in childhood can continue to exert negative effects on adults because these injuries influence thoughts, ideas, feelings, and actions in indirect and hidden ways. Many of the injuries could be from infancy and are buried in memory that cannot be accessed because they were not stored in a form that is understood after language is developed. This is somewhat like storing information in an early computer language that later computers cannot read because they don't have the old programs.

This chapter focuses on identifying and understanding some of the unproductive thoughts and feelings that can be a result of injuries experienced in childhood. We're focusing here on those thoughts and feelings that continue to influence you as an adult and that prevent you from developing a stronger and more cohesive self. The benefits of building this stronger self include the following:

- Increased self-confidence and self-esteem

- More constructive and satisfying interpersonal relationships that are meaningful and that endure

- Prevention of further injury by your self-absorbed parent

- Reduction of distressing and negative feelings overall, but most especially in interactions with your parent

- Becoming more centered and grounded

- Less susceptibility to reinjury because of nonconscious or unconscious faulty perceptions about your self

We'll also begin to examine a process for working with the more intense feelings you have around wounding events from your life. The lists you retained from exercise 2.1 will be used in the remainder of the book. You may think the focus should be on what was done to you and its unfairness. However, the approach used here focuses on what you can do to help yourself. This approach allows you to take control, become more effective, and understand the extent of your personal responsibility for what happens to you, now and in the future.

The basic assumptions underlying this approach are the following:

- Distressing events in your life were intensely wounding to your essential self.

- These past events and relationships continue to impact and influence your self-perception and some of your personal relationships.

- You are unable to release many negative and intense feelings related to these events.

- You cannot go back and change what happened to you.

- Other people, no matter how well-meaning they are or how much they want to help, cannot change the negative feelings you have.

- Apologies from others would not, or did not, lessen the negative feelings you carry.

- Time has not changed your feelings or perception of the events or people involved.

- You have a desire to lessen or let go of the negative feelings.

Thus, this approach focuses on you and how you can build your essential self to be strong so that you are less vulnerable to becoming reinjured by what your self-absorbed parent says and does, less sensitive to disparaging remarks and actions of others, and less likely to become isolated or alienated. It also asks you to reflect on whether you unconsciously have behaviors and attitudes reflective of a Destructive Narcissistic Pattern (DNP), where you exhibit considerable self-absorbed behaviors and attitudes, such as a lack of empathy, requiring constant attention or admiration, or an attitude of superiority and entitlement. These and other such behaviors and attitudes will prevent you from being able to form and maintain meaningful and satisfying relationships.

A strong and cohesive self will permit you to let go of some long-term hurts inflicted by your self-absorbed parent. Even a strong and cohesive self will not prevent you from *ever* being hurt, but it can make such events happen less often, reduce the intensity of your negative feelings, and allow you to more readily let go of the negativity. This alone is positive for your physical and emotional health and for the quality of your relationships.

A strong and cohesive self will allow you to do all of the following:

- Not personalize everything, or almost everything, others say and do

- More accurately judge external threats to yourself and thereby reduce your experience of anger and fear

- Understand if and when another person is displacing or projecting what she finds personally unacceptable onto you, and reject the displacement or projection, enabling you to reduce identifying with the projection

- More easily let go of minor irritations and annoyances

- Become more accepting of your imperfections while you continue to work on them

- Be happier with yourself and with others, helping you to develop and maintain meaningful and satisfying relationships

- Be warm, caring, and appropriately empathic with others

Although a major part of getting rid of old insults, hurts, and the like involves resolving and healing the wounds, the other major part is to further develop your self so that you become less susceptible to narcissistic wounding. Your self is better protected, more firmly grounded, appropriately defended, and not subject to others' assaults or manipulation. You become more in charge of what you allow to affect your self.

YOUR ATTITUDES AND BEHAVIORS

Let's get some sense of what attitudes and behaviors you have that may be further developed or eliminated to begin constructing a more cohesive and stronger self.

Assess yourself on the items below using the following ratings.

Thoughts and Feelings Scale

5—You always, or almost always, think or feel this way.

4—You frequently think or feel this way.

3—You sometimes think or feel this way.

2—You seldom think or feel this way.

1—You never, or almost never, think or feel this way.

1. When someone criticizes you, you feel ashamed for not being better. 5 4 3 2 1

2. When something doesn't go right at home or at work, you feel that others are blaming you for what happened. 5 4 3 2 1

3. You work hard to meet others' expectations and are disappointed in yourself when you fail or don't seem to meet them. 5 4 3 2 1

4. You feel that other people are pointing out your flaws and imperfections if they don't compliment or praise you. 5 4 3 2 1

5. It is difficult for you to shrug off or ignore irritations and annoyances. 5 4 3 2 1

6. You tend to catch other people's feelings, especially their negative feelings, such as anger, disgust, and sadness. 5 4 3 2 1

7. Your flaws and imperfections are a constant source of shame for you, and you seem to stay very aware of them. 5 4 3 2 1

8. It would be helpful if other people were more like you, working on their flaws and imperfections. 5 4 3 2 1

9. You wish that your relationships were more meaningful and satisfying. 5 4 3 2 1

10. Although you try to be warm, caring, and empathic with others, you get overwhelmed or enmeshed with their feelings, and that is very uncomfortable. 5 4 3 2 1

Scoring: Add your ratings to get a total score. Scores of 40 to 50 indicate that you are very susceptible to others' negative perceptions of you and give them unwarranted validity. Scores of 30 to 39 indicate much susceptibility; 20 to 29 indicate some susceptibility; 10 to 19 indicate a little susceptibility; and 0 to 9 indicate scant or no susceptibility.

Now let's take a look at some key attitudes and behaviors that can tend to undermine the development of a strong, cohesive self. We'll be working on these throughout the book.

Tending to Personalize

Have you ever been characterized as touchy or overly sensitive? Has someone told you that you took her comment as personal when it wasn't meant that way? Does this seem to frequently happen to you? Do you find that much of what others say seems to be pointing a finger of blame or criticism at you? Have you felt this way most or all of your life? If you are answering yes to many of these questions, and you rated yourself as 3 or above for item number 1 in the scale, then you have a tendency to personalize what others say and do.

When you personalize things, you feel that you are being criticized, blamed, and chastised for not being better or for not being good enough. That hurts, especially when coming from loved ones, when you feel it is unfair, and/or when it is about something over which you have no control or responsibility. It doesn't matter if the other person does not mean it that way; it only matters that you feel it that way. The validity of the seeming charge also does not matter, because you are more focused on your hurt and shame than you are on rationality and logic. Further, when someone tells you to not take it personally, that seems to only add to your distress.

This is one way that you continue to be reinjured, as there always seems to be someone to object to something, things don't go as planned, or you are the person who receives someone's displacement or projection. By taking these in and always personalizing them, you contribute to your reinjury. You have not yet learned or accepted the limits of your personal responsibility, accepted your personal limitations and strengths, or developed sufficient psychological boundary strength. This tendency also points to some self-absorption, where you want control over yourself, others, and events and think that you are the center of everyone's attention and expectations. Taking things personally can trigger or increase your feelings of shame, guilt, inadequacy, and fear. This is reason enough to try to curb this tendency.

Receiving Blame

There are many reasons why you can feel that others blame you when things go wrong.

- Others may openly say that you are to blame.

- You may have internalized an old parental message that continues to influence you today.

- One or more parents made you responsible for their psychological and/or physical welfare.

- You are a convenient scapegoat.

- Others find it easier to off-load blame, and you are available to take it in.

- You have unrealistic expectations for yourself.

There can be times when you feel blamed even though no one is saying so or doing anything that suggests that you are to blame. You take it on yourself and feel awful for whatever it was. A good example of this is how many parents feel they are to blame when their children fail or do something wrong. This feeling is not unusual and, in some instances, may even be correct; that is, the parent is to blame, in part. The same may be true for you in other ways. That is, you do bear some responsibility for what happened, but not the entire responsibility. However, you blame yourself for all of it.

Taking responsibility for your actions is a very good thing and is a behavior and attitude to be cultivated. On the other hand, if you rated yourself as 3 or higher on item number 2, you may perceive yourself as being blamed when no blame is intended, when you have unrealistic expectations for yourself, or when you don't have a good grasp of the limits of your influence, power, and control.

Then, too, there can be times when you are unfairly being blamed for something, but you still take it in as your responsibility. Others don't want the blame, so they seek ways to make sure they don't get it. You aren't able to defend yourself adequately, so the blame gets loaded onto you. It is very frustrating when something like that happens, and you may find that you act inappropriately out of your frustration. When you do, others can charge that you are being defensive, overreacting, or refusing to take responsibility. The more you try to protest, explain, or defend yourself, the more it seems like you are the right person to blame. And so it goes, with you becoming more and more frustrated and feeling increasingly inadequate. You may even regress some and behave as you did when unfairly blamed by a parent or sibling. This sequence can then lead to other feelings—shame, guilt, and fear.

Disappointing Others and Yourself

Rating yourself 3 or higher on item number 3 can suggest that you have unrealistic expectations for and perceptions of yourself like the following:

- You are supposed to please others.

- It is your responsibility to see to it that others are not disappointed.

- Other people's needs and desires are more important than yours.

- You become profoundly disappointed in yourself for not being better than you are.

- You tend to assume that others are disappointed when they are not and that you are at fault.

- When someone expresses displeasure or disappointment, you assume that person had expectations of you that you failed to meet.

It would be helpful if you could reserve your disappointment in yourself for those times when you really failed to live up to your personal standards, ethics, morals, or values. It is also helpful when you vow to not repeat that act again, take steps to understand your behavior, and use your disappointment to make needed changes instead of beating up on yourself or repressing, denying, or rationalizing what you did.

Your basic responsibility is to live up to your standards, and if that pleases others, their approval is icing on the cake. You don't have a responsibility to always or almost always please others, and you don't have a responsibility to act in a way just to avoid disappointing someone else. It is also true that others don't have a responsibility to act so that you are not disappointed. Act in accord with yourself and you will not experience this kind of guilt and shame. You may be sad or regretful when someone is disappointed, but you will not be disappointed in yourself.

Expecting Compliments and Praise

Are you a person who requires positive feedback and kind words in order to know and feel that you are behaving as expected or meeting others' approval, or that others like you? Is it wounding when you don't get these? Do you then feel that you weren't good enough or you would have been complimented and praised? Receiving some acknowledgment of your competence, efforts, and the like is most always appreciated, but a constant need for these can indicate a requirement for reassurance. This is especially true when you interpret a lack of compliments and praise as the other person pointing out your flaws and imperfections. You are using an absence (no positive feedback) to infer a positive (that they mean to indicate that you are flawed and imperfect).

If you rated yourself as 3 or higher on item number 4, then you may be very easily wounded by this irrational thought or belief. You may already be painfully aware of what you consider your flaws, hoping that others don't see them and needing compliments and praise to offset them. Failure to receive positive strokes leads to more wounding.

Compliments and praise can become empty and meaningless when they are insincere, constantly extended for minor things, or given because you expect them. In these circumstances, they fail to satisfy your need, and you may then extend yourself even further to get the feedback you require. You may think that your flaws and imperfections are obvious, and that's why you are not receiving what you need.

You may be primarily focused on external validation and acceptance rather then on self-validation and self-acceptance. Your attempts to hide, mask, deny, repress, and rationalize what you think are imperfections consume a lot of energy that could be better used to build your self, promote your self-acceptance, and change whatever behavior and attitudes really do need changing.

Feeling Irritated and Annoyed

One characteristic you may have that helps prevent you from letting go of negative or distressing feelings is an inability to ignore minor irritations and annoyances. Staying aware of what you are feeling can be very good for you. For example, knowing when you are irritated or annoyed can permit you to deal with that mild feeling to prevent escalation to a more intense feeling of anger. However, once you are aware of being irritated or annoyed, you have an opportunity to reflect on your feeling, judge the threat to yourself, and realize that you don't have to keep the feeling if you don't want to. If you don't let go at this point, the irritations and annoyances keep building up and festering so that they can jump to anger at any time.

Your inability to overlook, ignore, or let go of minor irritations and annoyances can be traced, in part, to what you think the triggering acts are saying about you. You become irritated or annoyed when you sense a threat to yourself. This is the first step in becoming actually angry, where the body prepares itself for fight or flight. However, most irritating and annoying acts present no real threat and can be overlooked or ignored. For instance, your wife or husband folding your clothes in a sloppy way is not a realistic threat to your core self. Further, holding on to these annoyances can have negative effects on your health, sense of well-being, and relationships.

If you rated yourself as 3 or higher on item number 6, try the following exercise to get started on thinking of ways you can ignore minor irritations and annoyances.

Exercise 3.1: Irritations and Annoyances

Materials: A sheet of paper and a pen or pencil for writing

Procedure: Find a place to work where you will not be disturbed.

1. Sit in silence and think of a recent event that produced irritation or annoyance for you. Nothing major, just something small, but you still can feel some discomfort when you think about it.

2. Recall what was done or said and write a sentence or brief paragraph that describes the irritating or annoying act. If you experienced something unspoken or not observable, like an attitude, try to capture that in a few words.

3. Now list what the act or attitude seemed to be saying about you. Don't focus on the other person, the validity of what was done or said, the right or wrong, and so on. Stay focused on what you thought or felt it said about you. You can also select from the following list if any fit:

   ■ I'm stupid.

   ■ I'm disgraceful.

   ■ I'm not good enough.

   ■ I'm not loved.

- I'm not valued.

- I'm not in control.

- I'm powerless.

- I'm helpless.

- I'm hopeless.

- I'm not appreciated.

- I'm not worthwhile.

- I'll be hurt, abandoned, or destroyed.

4. Give whatever you listed in step 3 a validity rating from 0 (no validity) to 10 (extreme validity), that is, how true this statement is about you. For example, if you wrote or chose "I'm stupid" as what the act or attitude seemed to be saying about you, you now rate the extent to which you think "I'm stupid" actually fits you.

5. Low validity ratings indicate that what you perceived the act or attitude to say about you is not how you perceive yourself. If you feel that there is little or no validity to the charge, you then need to ask yourself, "Why am I reacting to an untruth about me?" If the thought you were operating under at the time is really false, you can overlook or ignore it. It doesn't matter, and it doesn't fit.

6. If you are still bothered even though you gave it a low validity rating, you may want to explore for yourself if you have a suspicion that there is some truth to what the act seems to be saying about you. You may also have that perception about yourself, which the annoying event seemed to confirm. The same can be true if you gave it a moderate or high validity rating. This is something to work on, but you don't have to retain the irritation or annoyance.

Catching Others' Feelings

Do you find that you become distressed or upset when you are in the presence of someone who is sad, despairing, or otherwise upset? If you're around someone who is hostile or angry, do you become tense, say sarcastic things, or become curt and abrupt in your responses? Do you want to get away when interacting with someone who is emotionally intense and find that you retain some anxiety even after leaving her? These are examples of how you can experience catching others' emotions. Your psychological boundary strength is not sufficiently strong and resilient enough to keep you from becoming enmeshed or overwhelmed by others' emotions.

If you rated yourself as 3 or higher on item number 5 on the scale, then you may be contributing to your injury or reinjury by taking in others' pain, resentment, anger, fear, and the like. You tend to catch these feelings, they stay with you, you resonate with them, and you become injured or reinjured. You are personalizing and identifying with someone else's feelings and find it difficult or impossible to separate your feelings from hers and let them go, so you remain mired.

Building your psychological boundaries will enable you to not catch others' feelings. You will be able to be empathic, but you will not incorporate or identify with their feelings. You will also be able to let them have their feelings without falling prey to any of the following:

- Taking the feelings into your self and identifying with them

- Remaining mired in unpleasant feelings and unable to let go

- Feeling that you are responsible for the other person's welfare when she is capable of taking care of herself

- Trying to make the feelings go away for the other person so that she will feel better, allowing you to feel better also

■ Becoming upset yourself

Developing strong and resilient boundaries is a process, and you may want to use the expertise and guidance of a competent therapist to work with you on this. My book *Whose Life Is It Anyway? When to Stop Taking Care of Their Feelings and Take Care of Your Own* (2002) could give you some understanding of where your boundaries could be stronger and more resilient and can start you on the process of developing better boundary strength. Some material in *Children of the Self-Absorbed* relates to boundary strength and also addresses other self concerns.

Feeling Flawed and Imperfect

Everyone has flaws and imperfections, but for a child of a self-absorbed parent, these perceived flaws can be a considerable source of guilt, shame, and pain. Perceived flaws and imperfections may be realistic or irrational. An example of the latter is when someone feels she has to be perfect in everything, and so when the inevitable happens and she does something that's not perfect, she takes that as an opportunity to berate herself. This dynamic is in effect even when that person cognitively knows that perfection is an ideal and that most mistakes are not shameful. She knows it, but she doesn't feel it.

Getting in touch with your flaws can set off some powerful emotions that go to the core of your self. After all, it is your essential self that defines you as a person, and you want to be proud of who you are. This is what everyone wants. Accepting that you have flaws and imperfections is a lifelong process that some people never really begin. They may say that they are self-accepting, but the reality is that they deny, repress, hide, and mask their true self because of what they perceive as unacceptable imperfections. On the other hand, if you rated item 7 on the scale as 3 or higher, you don't hide these from yourself; you are painfully aware of them, and this causes you some distress. You are constantly reminded that you have flaws and imperfections, but you also don't seem to be able to do what seems necessary to overcome them. This also causes you some distress.

If this characterization fits you, then you probably find it difficult to forgive others and impossible to forgive yourself for any lapses, mistakes, failures, and so on. You are as hard and demanding of others as you are of yourself and wonder why others don't work harder to overcome their flaws and imperfections. Your flaws make you miserable, and you do and say things that let others know you are miserable and/or that you don't approve of them because of their flaws and imperfections. You are really taken aback when others don't get upset at being wrong, making errors, and the like. You don't understand how they can be so accepting of being less than perfect, because you can't do that.

A major part of building your self will be to become more self-accepting. That doesn't mean that you give up working to become a better person—it means that you have a different attitude and perception of yourself. You are able to focus on your strengths and positive attributes even though you remain aware of your flaws and imperfections. The first part is what you lack now, and this is one of the reasons why your flaws and imperfections are a constant source of pain and shame. You are minimizing your good points and allowing what you perceive as negative to dominate your thoughts and self-acceptance. You'll learn some strategies to help with this imbalance in later chapters.

Needing Others to Be Like You

Although you may be aware of your flaws and imperfections, you are also proud of some of your behaviors and attitudes if you rated yourself 3 or higher for item 8. You wish that others had some of your characteristics because that would mean that you are not flawed and that the following statements are true:

- You were correct and are validated.

- You would not have to correct what others do or say.

- You would feel safer or rest easier.

- You know that things would be done as they should be done.

- You would not have to clean up others' mistakes, errors, and failures.

- You could be confident that things were okay.

You may secretly think and feel that your way is the right way, and the world would be a better place if people could only bring themselves to behave, think, and feel more like you do. All this could be true; you probably do have many behaviors and attitudes that deserve praise, you could be a role model in many ways, and you do see how others could improve and be less troublesome. You work hard, do your best to take care of your responsibilities, do what you can to take care of others, are polite and kind, and so on. You have many positive characteristics and should be proud about these parts of yourself.

However, your thoughts about others being more like you can open you to injury when others don't seem to want those behaviors and attitudes, openly reject your attempts to get them to change, and don't find these characteristics as admirable as you do. It can feel like others are devaluing, dismissing, disparaging, or rejecting you, not just choosing to think, feel, and behave in other ways. It is painful to feel that your self is rejected, and you don't see why they don't want to be more like you. Your reactions can range from shame about yourself for being devalued to rage and resentment about the person who is refusing to acknowledge that yours is a better and a more desirable way to be. Your reaction influences how you perceive and relate to that person.

What would be helpful for you is to recognize and accept that you cannot cause others to change, that there are other laudable attitudes and ways to behave, that others can find their own way to more constructive behaviors and attitudes, and that not being like you does not necessarily mean that others are wrong, bad, inept, or shameful. You will become less wounded when you can accept and appreciate others, even when they are different from you. This can be a major shift for you, but you can reduce and eliminate some of your wounding without giving up any of your admirable qualities.

Maintaining Meaningful and Satisfying Relationships

All relationships can go through some rough spots where you question commitment, purpose, meaningfulness, or its degree of satisfaction. You question these because of many factors and conditions, such as the following:

- You become old enough and able to live apart from your parents.

- Your best friend gets married.

- You graduate from high school or college.

- You move to another city for a better job.

- You unexpectedly come into a lot of money.

- A child or a partner becomes seriously ill.

- You or your partner are in the military.

- You are assigned to a war zone.

- A friend goes to prison.

- A sibling becomes chemically dependent and refuses treatment.

The list of such circumstances is long. Another thing that can trigger you to question a relationship is a feeling of dissatisfaction. The dissatisfaction can be with yourself, the other person, conditions at work, or even life circumstances. You can begin to question your relationships for many and varied reasons. What is most important, however, is that your satisfaction and the relationship's meaningfulness be a part of your awareness. Take a moment and do the following exercise.

Exercise 3.2: My Relationships

Materials: Several sheets of paper, a pen or pencil for writing, and a set of crayons, felt markers, or colored pencils

Procedure: Find a place to complete the exercise where you will not be disturbed and can work in comfort.

1. Make a list of your current relationships by role or category, such as mother, aunt, peers at work, bosses, lover or spouse, and children. Use names if that is more useful for you. Be sure to include relationships that may have some distance but where there is still a connection.

2. On another sheet of paper, write the name of each person across the bottom of the page, then draw a vertical line on the left side of the page. Put numbers on the line beginning with 0 at the bottom of the line and 100 at the top. Place other numbers, such as 10, 20, and so on, between 0 and 100. Then draw a bar graph from each name to the number on the vertical line that illustrates the quality of that relationship, using a different color for each bar. The quality (vertical line of the bar) should range from 0 for low quality to 100 for ideal quality.

3. Review your graph and write a brief statement about the quality of each relationship, noting what you can do to enhance the quality or if you even want to improve the relationship.

4. The final step is to make a list of the relationships that you can enhance, repair, or develop. If there are some you wish or need to discard, draw a line through these. If there are some that you feel are hopeless and you have to endure for some reason, highlight these with one of the colors. This is your plan for developing

your relationships. The strategies and suggestions provided in this book to build your self, reduce self-absorbed behaviors and attitudes, and develop healthy adult narcissism will also contribute to your ability to form and maintain meaningful, satisfying, and enduring relationships.

Becoming Overwhelmed and Enmeshed

You can be wounded when your psychological boundaries are not sufficiently developed and fortified to prevent you from becoming overwhelmed or enmeshed with other people's feelings. If you rated item number 10 as 3 or higher, you extend yourself to be warm, caring, and empathic only to often find that you are left feeling distressed, inadequate, despairing, angry, and full of other negative feelings. This is an indication that you are unable to maintain your sense of yourself as separate and distinct from others when you try to be empathic. You become lost or taken over by the other person's feelings. This state can leave you open to considerable wounding, especially when you then incorporate the other person's feelings and identify with them on an unconscious level. You don't realize what's happening until it's too late, if ever, and you're left with those feelings.

Boundary strength refers in part to your deep understanding of your self as separate and distinct from others. This understanding is developed over time and its development is significantly influenced by parental actions and attitudes during your early years. Examples of these attitudes and behaviors that contribute to incomplete separation and individuation are the following:

- Overprotection or underprotection of the child

- Not permitting the child to have different choices and preferences from the parent

- The parent making the child responsible for the parent's psychological, emotional, and/or physical well-being

- The parent not supporting the child's choices or discouraging the child from making decisions

- Expecting the child to unmindfully accept and act on parental values, morals, ethics, and the like

Experiencing one or more of these can suggest that you may have incomplete separation and individuation that contribute to an unrealistic extension of self. This means that you can lack understanding of where you end and where others begin, the boundary that distinguishes you from others. This is one reason why you are not yet able to withstand others' emotions, especially when their emotions are intense, when they are powerful "senders" of their emotions, or when you have an especially close connection to the person. These factors enable you to more easily catch their feelings, and once caught, you incorporate them and make them yours. You may feel you are simply being empathic, but true empathy does not require you to take on the other person's feelings and make them yours. You can let go of these when your psychological boundaries are strong and resilient.

This topic is much too complex to adequately discuss here, and I encourage you to find out more about your psychological boundary strength through the guidance of a competent mental health therapist and/or through further reading and self-reflection. Developing complete separation and individuation is a lifelong process needing constant attention. However, the payoff is well worth the effort.

UNDERSTANDING YOUR CONTRIBUTIONS

If you've read and completed the scales and exercises in this chapter, you now have some understanding of how you can or do contribute to your wounding. Yes, other people do say and do things that are mean, demeaning, and devaluing, but you don't have to let these enter and hurt you. You don't have to hold on to the words and actions, letting them fester and affect you and your relationships in unconscious ways. You can just remember them, but not permit them to continue to upset and wound you. You can understand why you get hurt, build your self to better withstand these kinds of assaults, and let go of the negative feelings.

As I discussed before, the depth and extent of your narcissistic wounding is related to your early life events that produced the initial wounding. You may not have words to describe these events, nor may you even remember them. That's not important for what this book is trying to do. Even if you could remember them, you cannot change them. The best you could do is to understand what happened and realize that these experiences don't have to continue to negatively affect you. The approach used here is to understand what kinds of events could have produced your initial wound, suggest how your current behavior and attitudes may contribute to your injury or re-injury, propose steps and techniques for personal development of your self, and provide a process for letting go. The work you've done so far in this book is the beginning of this process, and we will continue to develop skills and understanding to help you better manage these old scars and prevent further wounding.

CHAPTER 4

Difficult Situations and How to Cope

Difficult situations in which your negative feelings are triggered are more about you than they are about the other person. A primary response you may be using for these situations is to try to get the other person to change, which, in the case of the self-absorbed parent, does not work. However, the failure seldom deters you from continuing this futile effort. This parent will not change because you want him to change, does not accept that he needs to change, thinks that you're the one who needs to change, and is not reluctant to continually point this out to you, thereby exacerbating the effect on you. You will be much more effective and serene when you can accept that the parent will not change, when you build your self to be less unconsciously dependent on your parent, and when you are more centered, grounded, strong, and resilient.

Your feelings can be managed, whether they arise from within you or are projected by someone else and you incorporate and act on them. You can control what you feel, the feeling's intensity, and whether or not to verbalize or otherwise act on your feelings. You have more power over your feelings than you may think, and this power can help you navigate difficult situations and events with your self-absorbed parent. This chapter begins with some information about emotions so that you can begin to understand why you feel as you do and what you can do to control and manage your feelings, especially the negative ones that can be triggered by your self-absorbed parent. This understanding is basic to using the strategies you'll be learning later that can assist you in difficult situations.

WHY YOU FEEL AS YOU DO

Feelings are a collection of sensations that your thoughts interpret and label, usually in relation to your self and its welfare. These sensations can be initiated by external and internal events, people, situations, and the like, but it is your interpretations of these that determine what you feel. Most of this occurs on a nonconscious or unconscious level, and the factors contributing to your interpretations may not be fully understood.

Let's examine the factors that go into your feelings: sensations, interpretations, and the factors that influence these interpretations. Sensations result from stimuli, either internal or external. These sensations are subjected to personal interpretations that are most often focused on the well-being of the self, and those interpretations are collected or collapsed into a labeled feeling. For example, your feel angry when your self is in danger of becoming overwhelmed, enmeshed, or destroyed. The collection of sensations when angry include muscular tension, elevated blood pressure, rapid pulse, a surge of adrenaline, and shallow breathing as the body prepares for fight or flight from the perceived danger. Once the body prepares, the interpretation of internal or external factors leads to the label of "anger." (The same process seems to be true for fear.) The influential factors of personality, family-of-origin experiences, and past experiences interact to produce the interpretation and assessment of the potential threat to the well-being of the self.

Your analysis and interpretation of the sensations and the well-being of the self also lead to the decision about the resulting label for the feeling. For example, the interpretation of a threat to the self could lead to the feeling of irritation or annoyance rather than the related but more intense feeling of anger.

Being around your self-absorbed parent can trigger your old childhood feelings, such as helplessness, fear, inadequacy, and the like. Although you are now an adult and react differently with other people, you may be unable to do so when you are in the presence of your parent, or even on the phone. In these instances, you may regress (go back) to feeling and reacting as you did in earlier interactions, during your childhood. What can be more troubling to you and your relationships today is that you may be unconsciously reacting to what others say or do, or what you *perceive* them to be saying or doing, as being similar to your parent. This is transference: a reaction to others that is not consistent with current reality but is consistent with the past relationship with your parent. We will discuss more about transference later. But, before we tackle the emotions your self-absorbed parent triggers, let's do an exercise that can help keep you from reexperiencing those intense and negative feelings that may emerge as you read and recall some events.

Exercise 4.1: The Calm Within You

Materials: A set of crayons, felt markers, or colored pencils and one or more sheets of paper for drawing, and a hard surface for drawing

Procedure. Read all steps before beginning to work. Find a place to sit and draw where you will be free from interruptions or distractions.

1. Sit in silence, close your eyes, and allow your breathing to become deep and even. Do this for approximately one minute or longer.

2. Think of a scene where you could or did feel peaceful, calm, and at ease. The scene can be real or imaginary.

3. Stay with the scene and notice as many details as possible.

4. When you have the scene as you want it, open your eyes and draw it. Art expertise or talent is not necessary—whatever you produce is acceptable. Give your drawing a title.

5. This scene can be your inner calm place, and is immediately accessible at any time. All you have to do is to think of the title or recall the image. It can take only seconds to go to your inner place of calmness in the future, because all you have to do is to visualize this scene.

You can use this image any time you feel troubled and uncomfortable. Because we will be reviewing some difficult experiences and feelings as we proceed in this book, I suggest you use your calming scene whenever you feel uncomfortable as you read. When you feel unpleasant or scary emotions start to build, take a moment to close your eyes and imagine your calm image. The scene can also be used in interactions with your self-absorbed parent when you find that you are becoming upset. It may be helpful to practice retrieving the calming scene as much as possible, as this practice can make it easier and faster to access.

DIFFICULT SITUATIONS

There are numerous difficult situations you may encounter with your self-absorbed parent, each unique to you and to your situation. It isn't feasible to try to present all such situations—they can be as varied as each person's experience. So, for ease of discussion, I'll group these situations into different categories, listed below:

- Injuring attacks on your self

- Conflicts

- Unreasonable demands and intrusive questions

- Holidays and other celebrations

- The aging, dependent parent

■ Boundaries and protection for your children

Because your personality and needs are unique to you, I won't be presenting specific strategies for each category. After we discuss each category and what makes it difficult, I'll provide a number of general strategies to choose from. Select the ones that best fit you and that you think you can implement.

Injuring Attacks on Your Self

These attacks are criticism, blame, and devaluing and demeaning comments. They are injuring because they point out how the speaker perceives your self and do so in very unflattering terms. There may even be unfair comparisons of you with other people, as if they are better or more acceptable. Examples of such comments include the following:

■ "Why can't you ever (get it right, be more successful, look better, dress well, keep your hair fixed, and so on)?"

■ "You never/you always…"

■ "You ought to know (do, be, and so forth) better than that (this)."

■ "You're just no good, and I tried my best with you."

■ "Your (sister, brother, cousin, acquaintance) can do (something). Why can't you be more like him or her?"

■ "I don't know what to do with you. You're such a (mess, ingrate, difficult child)."

■ "You always get it wrong."

■ "Don't be such a crybaby (wimp, drip, nerd, and so on)."

Conflicts

Conflicts can range from mild disagreements to battles. The most important point about conflicts is how they leave you feeling. Generally, conflicts with your self-absorbed parent arouse feelings that leave you upset, helpless, ineffective, and wrong or inadequate. Think about it. Have you ever come out of such a conflict, even a mild one, feeling like a winner? Your answer is probably either no or seldom. You've also probably tried everything to avoid these conflicts, to get your parent to see your perspective, or to make him aware of the impact he has on you in the hope that he would care enough to refrain from hurtful comments. However, your efforts have not produced the desired results, but this failure may not prevent you from continuing to try.

While all the strategies discussed later in this chapter can be used, there are others that are very suitable for conflict situations with your self-absorbed parent, such as the following.

Avoid conflicts. When you want to challenge your parent about something or respond to his challenge, institute the following:

1. Assess the importance of your "winning."

2. Even if winning is important for you, there are other, more significant "wins," and you can focus on these. Examples include developing a loving family of your own, having a rich and meaningful life, enhancing your creativity, and other positive achievements.

3. Smile and fog the situation. "Fogging" means to obscure the discussion. Tactics for fogging include changing the topic, focusing on an irrelevancy, bringing something offbeat into the conversation, and so on.

4. Become distracted, such as needing a bathroom break, checking with the babysitter, remembering something needed or to be taken care of that you left in the car or at home (always

try to leave something—important or unimportant). Any distraction will suffice.

Don't bring others into the fray. When you try to include others, it makes them uncomfortable and doesn't provide the support you were seeking.

Seek support for your position later from someone like a friend or therapist. Some time and distance can provide you with an opportunity to be more self-reflective, reduce some emotional intensity, and use your self-affirmations. If you feel that you need support for your position, such as reassurance that you are right and your parent is wrong, explore this with a valued confidant and/or therapist who can maintain confidentiality.

Don't show your feelings at this time—keep them private. Use your emotional insulation to prevent revealing your feelings at this time, because revealing them will not be helpful and can even be harmful to you. Your parent has never been moved by your feelings and may have turned them against you to make you appear even more wrong or inadequate, and you have usually left feeling worse. Nothing has changed with your parent that would lead you to believe that your feelings will matter to him.

If your parent makes errors of fact, gently and calmly correct these once and say no more about the errors. He will be unable to admit his errors, and your continuing to belabor the point will not make him do so and is likely to arouse his ire.

Let your parent have his perspective. Mentally shrug your shoulders. Physically shrugging your shoulders in his presence may only inflame him. Don't contest him because you cannot win, and engaging in a contest only makes things worse for you. Try adopting an attitude that there are various perspectives for any situation; you have one, and your parent has another. You want to keep yours, and he can keep his.

The other strategies you'll encounter in the book can also help prepare you to become more effective in handling conflicts with your parent.

Unreasonable Demands and Intrusive Questions

Your self-absorbed parent may still expect you to be at his beck and call, even though you are an adult and have a life and responsibilities separate from him. He may make unreasonable demands on you to do things he can do for himself, to be responsible for his physical and emotional welfare, to always do what he wants you to do or to be what he wants you to be, to act on his desires and wishes, and to accept his authority without dissent. He seems to think that your responsibilities, such as a job or family time, should be secondary to whatever he thinks or wants. You may try to meet as many of his expectations and demands as you possibly can, but you can never give him enough, and trying to meet his demands may even be detrimental to other parts of your life.

Both unreasonable demands and intrusive questions show a lack of understanding and respect for your boundaries. Further, both put you in a position where you run the risk of offending if you do not immediately comply and do what is wanted or supply the desired answers. Intrusive questions are those that ask for intimate, personal, and sensitive information about yourself or others that you may not want to share. When faced with questions like these, you may need time to understand your own needs, desires, and wishes, and when engaged in an interaction, you cannot take the time you need. You are too busy interacting and reacting. These types of questions can be used to put you on the defensive, to illustrate how wrong or inadequate you are in some respect, and other such negative goals. The most irritating thing about intrusive questions is that there is unconscious internal pressure as well as external pressures to provide answers when questions are asked. It can be difficult to ignore or refuse to answer these, especially when they come from a parent.

Part of the problem with parental unreasonable demands and intrusive questions is the parent's inability or unwillingness to accept you as separate and distinct from him. When he makes these demands, he fails to understand that you are a functioning adult to be related to as an adult, and he is exhibiting self-absorbed attitudes of entitlement and exploitation. On your side, you may still be relating to your parent as if you were a child, feel the need to comply with his demands or answer his questions, and not know how to set reasonable limits for him to relate and behave with you. Mostly what you are dealing with are your feelings about disappointing your parent, not being a "good child," and being perceived as rude or disrespectful. These are difficult feelings to overcome to the extent where you are able to refuse unreasonable demands, comply with reasonable ones to the best of your ability, and refuse to answer intrusive questions while still sharing something of your life. Some of the suggestions provided later in this chapter and in the remainder of the book may be helpful, but some challenges may need help from a competent therapist to build and fortify your self to attain more complete separation and individuation.

Holidays and Other Celebrations

Do you have a fantasy about family holidays and other celebrations that involves your self-absorbed parent? Do you hope each time that your image will be fulfilled and that you will look back on the event with warm and fond memories, only to never have this happen? Does your self-absorbed parent manage to do or say something every time to spoil the occasion for you? Spoilers can include the following:

- Criticizing your looks; dress; job; spouse, lover, partner, or of lack of one; your plans or dreams for the future; how much money you make—the list is endless

- Blaming you for any irritation, error, or the like made by anyone, especially for any distress or inconvenience for the parent

- Making disparaging remarks about your opinions, ideas, and so on

- Unfairly comparing you with others in order to highlight your perceived inadequacies

- Resorting to name-calling, labeling, and put-downs

- Resurrecting old grudges, unpleasant events, and the like

- Saying provocative things to try to get you upset (and unfortunately, these usually work)

You probably have more examples to add to the list.

Although you continue to hope that your fantasy will come true, it never has. But you still long for a good outcome and continue to attend holiday and other celebratory events with the self-absorbed parent. Using some or all of the suggestions later in this chapter can begin to make these events more tolerable for you. However, what will be of most help is for you to give up the fantasy and yearning for meaningful changes in your parent.

The Aging, Dependent, Self-Absorbed Parent

An aging, dependent parent is one of the most difficult situations you can encounter, because his self-absorption can become more acute because of real conditions, such as failing health or finances. Even under the best of circumstances, these conditions and concerns can be troubling for parents and their children. The self-absorbed parent can ratchet up the complaints, unreasonable demands, blame, and criticism. The lack of empathy and concern for the adult child's circumstances only adds to the distressful situation, and the parent's entitlement attitude can really exacerbate all problems.

Added to the parent's self-absorbed behavior and attitude can be your guilt, feelings of inadequacy, anger, and resentment, and your own lingering aspects of undeveloped narcissism. These, too, are difficult to experience and manage effectively. You self comes under even greater assault as you try to deal with internal and external forces that surround the situation with the aging, dependent, self-absorbed parent. There are several points to remember when you are faced with these circumstances:

- Your parent does have some real problems with which he needs assistance.

- The parent becomes less able to cope with his life tasks, and this is distressful for him.

- The parent can be extremely fearful about what the future holds and fear having inadequate personal and/ or financial resources to deal with it.

- The loss, or potential loss, of independence is very upsetting and frightening.

- The parent is not likely to change and become less self-absorbed.

- The roles of child and parent become reversed, unless the child had already been put in the position of being responsible for the parent's welfare, such as what happens for the parentified child described in chapter 1.

Under these circumstances, it is extremely difficult to set limits on the extent of your responsibility and to feel that your actions are adequate. The most disstressing part is your resulting feelings, so you will have to recognize that you do have personal limits and realize what they are. You must avoid letting your lingering aspects of grandiosity (an aspect of undeveloped narcissism) color your thoughts and attitudes, convincing you that you must "fix" the problem, make it go away, or fully and completely satisfy your self-absorbed parent.

Boundaries for Your Children

This section is included because of the questions I have received from readers about this issue. They want to know how to protect their children from experiencing what they did, and they fear that the self-absorbed grandparent will now negatively affect their children. Just as your parent did not recognize your personal psychological boundaries, thought of you as an extension of him, exploited and manipulated you, was not empathic, and so on, he may now exhibit the same behaviors and attitudes with his grandchildren.

The good news is that the grandparent will have less of an effect on the grandchildren, unless you are living in the same home with your parent. Distance, less contact, and your interventions can do much to moderate the negative effects on your children. Your empathy and understanding of what your children experience with your self-absorbed parent will be supportive and insulating for them. You can insulate your child from harm by making empathic responses to the child that demonstrate your understanding of his feelings. This is not taking your child's side against your parent—it is affirming and supporting your child. Other strategies include the following:

- Communicate clear directions to your parent about how you want your child treated. For example, let your parent know that any transgression should be brought to your attention for proper treatment, and the grandparent should not punish or chide the child. Make sure the child also knows this.

- Block demeaning, blaming, critical comments and remarks, even if you have to take the heat yourself. You can block these by intervening and changing the topic, sending the child away to do or get something, interrupting your parent to praise your child for something, and other such behaviors. It will do no good to ask your parent to not make these remarks and comments.

- Insist on the child apologizing *only* when absolutely necessary, not to keep the peace. Keep such apologies to a minimum.

- Praise your child frequently in your parent's presence.

- Keep requests for babysitting or child management to a minimum, if you make them at all.

- Be pleasant and cordial, but stand up and support your child.

- If the parent starts to compare your child with anyone, immediately block it.

SPECIFIC STRATEGIES TO HELP

Presented below are general strategies that can be used with all types of self-absorbed parents. First are three internal states to reduce or eliminate. Second are four actions *not* to take, and third are constructive acts that can be helpful in difficult situations.

Reduce Your Vulnerability

First, do your best to reduce or eliminate the following:

- Your yearning and longing for your parent to show empathy, liking, and love for you

- Wishing that your parent would change

- Your emotional susceptibility

You may be able to reduce your yearning, longing, and wishing by becoming aware that these states are the roots for some, or much, of the discomfort you experience with your self-absorbed parent. Much pain will disappear when you can accept that your parent is unlikely to become the parent of your dreams, is unlikely to change, and sees no need for changing. The reality is that your longing, yearning, and wishing is futile. This doesn't mean that your parent doesn't love you. It does mean that he doesn't and can't love you in the way that you want or need. So, if the parent will not change, you can change.

You may not be able to help being emotionally susceptible with your parent, even if you have a rebellious response rather than a compliant one. Emotional susceptibility means that you are open to catching other people's feelings and may then also act on these as if they were your own. As we saw earlier in the book, catching others' feelings and acting on them is what is known as projective identification. An example could be when you become angry and cannot let go of the anger after an interaction with your parent. If this is projective identification, then what happened is that the parent projected his unwanted anger on to you, you caught the anger and internalized it on top of your existing irritation or fear, and then you began to act on it by becoming angry and unable to let this feeling go.

Reduction of emotional susceptibility can take some time and effort to achieve, but it's well worth the effort. Working with a therapist to build and fortify your psychological boundaries is a long-term strategy. Using the nonverbal techniques described later in this chapter can be helpful in the short term. These nonverbal techniques will reduce the likelihood of your positioning yourself to catch the parent's feelings and then unconsciously incorporating and acting on them. You may think that you have too much empathy, or that you are too sensitive, but it is much more likely that you are emotionally susceptible to unconsciously catching others' feelings and do not have sufficient psychological boundary strength. Boundary strength can be built, but it takes time and effort, and you need something to use in the interim. The strategies described here should be helpful.

Actions to Avoid

This next set of suggestions is focused on actions that you will want to work hard to avoid. These may be tempting to use because they can be a part of who you are or may provide some short-term satisfaction. Please do not use any of the following:

- Retaliation

- Empathizing

- Confrontation

- Disclosure of intimate thoughts and feelings

These do not help either the situation, your relationship with your self-absorbed parent, or your feelings about yourself. They are counterproductive and are not constructive for your growth and development.

RETALIATING

Retaliation occurs when you are hurt and do or say something designed to make the other person hurt as you were hurt. The short-term satisfaction does not last, the act can make the relationship worse, and, in the end, you haven't gained anything. The best retaliation or revenge is to build your self and to become successful in your accomplishments and achievements. This is much more constructive and is also personally satisfying.

EMPATHIZING

Empathy is a deep resonance with another's experience without losing your sense of self as separate and distinct from the other person. This ability is a characteristic of healthy adult narcissism, and its lack is a characteristic of the Destructive Narcissistic Pattern (DNP). Your parent probably does not empathize with you, and you may keenly feel this lack and long for your parent to be empathic. This may lead you to feel that you should, or must, empathize with your parent. You may even think that your empathy will help promote change in your parent. But when you try to empathize with your parent, you are more likely to open yourself up to incorporating your parent's negative projections and integrating these into your self, leaving you upset and unable to let go of the negative and uncomfortable feelings you've taken in. As a child of a parent with a DNP, you probably are especially vulnerable to this kind of emotion catching, and you may not have developed sufficient psychological boundary strength to prevent you from catching your parent's feelings, so it can be important for you to not empathize. If you want to do something, you can sympathize, where you make comforting and reassuring comments that don't require you to also experience the feelings that go along with the words.

CONFRONTING

I cannot emphasize enough the importance of not engaging in confrontation with your parent. Even if you are experienced in constructive confrontation, you would be ill-advised to try it with your self-absorbed parent. If you've made the attempt at a confrontation and you objectively and realistically recall the event, you are most likely to come to the realization that it didn't work. Not only was confrontation ineffective, but you were most likely left with residual negative feelings that lingered. You left the confrontation feeling worse than before you started. Your parent is not open to your thoughts, feelings, and ideas; does not relate to or care about your feelings; does not feel a need to change anything about himself; and can become enraged that you think that he is less than perfect. You cannot win, or even make any inroads into your parent's self-absorption.

DISCLOSING

You may have disclosed personal and intimate thoughts and feelings to your parent or may have been tempted to do so. This too is not advised because your parent is likely to use the information against you and your best interests. The results of disclosure can be that you are chastised or criticized, blamed for not being better, and accused (especially of disappointing the parent). You may be demeaned for your thoughts and feelings, and your parent may compromise the confidence of the material, telling others what you've shared and thus leading to more discord or criticism. Keeping mum about sensitive issues and feelings doesn't require you to cut your parent off from your personal life altogether, but it does mean that some of the following would be helpful:

- Tell your parent only what you wouldn't mind being revealed to the world.

- Don't take your problems or concerns to your parent. Find a trusted confidant who is knowledgeable and can keep a confidence.

- When talking with your parent, minimize any concerns or problems you may have. Be as upbeat as possible.

Helpful Actions

There are eight suggested actions that can help you with managing and controlling situations with your parent that can then help you contain and manage your unpleasant and difficult feelings. They are:

- Build and fortify your self.

- Block and control your feelings.

- Restrict interactions as much as possible, such as having most of these in a public place.

- Develop some self-affirmations.

- Use protective nonverbal behaviors.

- Choose what to feel.

- Interrupt your negative thoughts and feelings and substitute positive ones.

- Use self-talk to remind yourself of what is real and what is fantasy.

BUILD AND FORTIFY YOUR SELF

Building your self means that you develop empathy, creativity, inspiration, and relationships or connections. Doing so will enable you to let go of old grudges and resentments; have sufficient psychological boundary strength to lessen emotional susceptibility and judge what feelings are yours alone, uncontaminated with others' feelings; and better cope with your triggered feelings that are aroused in interactions with your self-absorbed parent. Chapter 9 presents some information to jump-start this process, and working with a therapist can facilitate the needed growth and development.

BLOCK AND CONTROL YOUR FEELINGS

There are strategies that can allow you to be calm when being blamed, criticized, demeaned, devalued, and the like so that you can think and act more constructively. The feelings are still there but can become less intense, which then makes them easier to put aside for the moment.

Blocking your emotions requires the following:

- An awareness of what you are experiencing, including the intensity of the feelings.

- A desire to avoid revealing or acting on these feelings.

- A personal strategy of momentarily disassociating from the feeling. Complete disassociation is not recommended, as this can produce or increase cutting off or distancing yourself from your feelings in all parts of your life. What could be helpful is a statement to yourself that you'll get back to the feelings when you are in a safer place.

- Using thoughts as expression rather than feelings. Thoughts are cognitive and easier to handle than are feelings, and you want to be in control for the time being.

For example, let's suppose that your parent has made a demeaning comment about your appearance, and you feel yourself becoming angry. Instead of staying with the anger and firing back at the parent or letting the anger move you to shame for disappointing the parent, it is at this point where you can mentally say that you don't want to act out of anger. You are going to choose to push the anger away for the moment, just act out of annoyance (a milder form of anger), and not let your parent know that the comment really angered you. So, you decide to make a noncommittal response, such as "Really? I'll need to pay better attention next time." You can also ignore the comment, change the topic, or make a pleasant comment about the parent's appearance. Any of these can defuse the situation and your anger.

RESTRICT INTERACTIONS

Another strategy is to make sure that most of your interactions with the parent that require more than a few minutes happen in public places, such as restaurants, entertainment venues, religious places of worship, and the like. It's usually easier for you to have your negative feelings triggered when interactions are prolonged, when they take place with intimate family members, like in holiday celebrations, or when you have to be alone with the parent. You can propose that events be held in public places; arrange any mandatory events, such as birthday parties, to include many nonfamily participants; and set reasonable time limits for your participation in these.

USE SELF-AFFIRMATIONS

Instead of getting caught up in intense negative emotions triggered by your self-absorbed parent, you can moderate and counteract these with self-affirmations. It can be important to remember that your triggered feelings are impacted when, on some level, you are buying into your parent's perceptions of you and fear that these have some validity. You may also find yourself in trouble when you are still engaged in the fantasy that your parent will magically change, or when you're feeling powerless to get your needs met. Self-affirmations remind you of your strengths and positive characteristics so that you don't get mired in thoughts and feelings about your real or imagined flaws.

Exercise 4.2: Develop Self-Affirmations

Materials: A 5 by 8-inch index card, a sheet of paper, and a pen or pencil for writing

Procedure: Find a quiet place to develop your affirmations where you will not be disturbed and where you'll have a hard surface for writing, such as a table or large book.

1. Use the sheet of paper to list ten to twelve things you consider to be your accomplishments, such as holding a job, overcoming an illness or condition, rearing responsible children, and so on.

2. Next to each accomplishment, list all personality characteristics associated with the accomplishment. For example, for holding a job you may list persistence, determination, ambition, organization, and so on.

3. Review the list of accomplishments and associations, and then construct another list that incorporates eight to ten personality characteristics that are repeated two or more times. These form the basis for your self-affirmations.

4. At the top of the index card, write "I am," and then write the list of repeated characteristics from step 3. These are your self-affirmations.

5. Read this card once a week until you can effortlessly recall the items *when you are experiencing intense negative emotions*, such as those experienced in interactions with your self-absorbed parent.

USE NONVERBAL BEHAVIORS

Some nonverbal signals of disassociation or disinterest can be of assistance. You are less likely to catch your self-absorbed parent's negative feelings or to have your negative feelings aroused if you can do any or all of the following:

- Avoid eye contact, especially sustained eye contact.

- Angle your body slightly or completely away from the parent.

- If forced to look at the parent, focus on his ear, his chin, or the middle of his forehead.

- Put some physical object between you and him. For example, turn a chair around so that the back faces the parent, or look at him over the top of some reading glasses.

- Adopt a relaxed body position. For instance, when seated, have your feet flat on the floor and arms and hands in an open position, and try to keep your breathing deep and even.

- Think about something pleasant or zone out.

- Keep a neutral or pleasant facial expression, but don't grin (or frown).

These behaviors are counterproductive for building relationships, showing interest, and communicating caring and concern, so they can effectively protect you from your parent's efforts to engage you. Try not to use nonverbal behaviors that are likely to arouse the parent's ire, such as those used by sullen adolescents (sulking, mumbling). You are not trying to get the parent angry, as that would increase his focus on you and can produce more negative comments. You are just trying to tolerate the situation for the moment.

CHOOSE WHAT TO FEEL

You may find it difficult to accept, but you do have choices about what to feel. It may appear to you that your feelings just emerge and that you have no control, but you do have the ability to decide what to feel, especially when you understand the roots of your feelings and have resolved some of your family-of-origin issues and past unfinished business. The negative feelings that you did not choose are triggered because of old parental messages that continue to affect your thoughts about the adequacy and acceptability of your self, thus setting off guilt and shame. These messages also impact your perceptions of your competency, efficacy, and lovability; your unconscious fears of abandonment or destruction; and your needs for liking and approval from the parent that are still lacking.

Don't get the idea that you should never experience feelings like shame. It can be growth enhancing to realize and accept your flaws, as long as there is also resolve and opportunity to address these. What we're talking about here is preventing your self-absorbed parent from setting your agenda for what you will feel, especially in interactions with him. The next two sections describe some strategies that can help with this, but first you have to understand and accept that you can choose what to feel, and that you do not have to feel what your parent is trying to inspire in you, catch the parent's negative feelings, or unconsciously react as you did when you were a child.

INTERRUPT NEGATIVE THOUGHTS
AND FEELINGS

Another strategy is to interrupt your negative thoughts about yourself. These can include self-criticism and blame, negative feelings such as shame and anger, and unrealistic ideas about yourself, such as the need for perfection. This strategy works best when you not only interrupt negative thoughts, but also substitute more positive thoughts, feelings, and ideas. When you are able to avoid having these negatives and can insert more positives, you become better able to tolerate interactions with your self-absorbed parent and will not be as vulnerable to getting mired in enduring and unpleasant thoughts and feelings about yourself. The self-affirmations you developed in exercise 4.2 can also be used here.

First, you need to become aware of when you are experiencing these negatives about yourself. For example, you may begin to experience them as you read this, perhaps feeling inadequate and flawed, or as you recall an incident with your parent where the unpleasant feelings continue to linger. You can practice interruption and substitution with these to experience what the outcomes may be. If you are experiencing some negatives at this point, stop reading and consciously interrupt any negative self-thoughts, ideas, and feelings. This includes any "should" and "ought" statements, such as "I should not let my parent get to me." These are unproductive and unhelpful. Next, substitute one of your positive self-affirmations or another positive self-statement. You may also want to remind yourself of the following:

- Others will not change because I want them to change.

- I do not have control over others' feelings, thoughts, and ideas.

- I don't have to fear being abandoned or destroyed, as I can take care of myself.

- I am independent, and others are too.

- When I think, feel, or imagine negatives about my self, that confirms my self-absorbed parent's perceptions.

- I have faults and flaws, as everyone does, but I am working to correct these.

- I have many positive attributes.

Practicing these kinds of positive and affirming statements when you're alone can pay off by making it easier to implement this strategy during interactions with your self-absorbed parent.

REMEMBER WHAT'S REAL

Use your self-talk to remind yourself of what is real and what is fantasy. The line between these can become blurred, especially when intense emotions are involved. Your negative feelings are easier to control when you can introduce some realism and not get caught up in fantasy. Try answering the following questions to get some idea of how fantasy interferes with reality:

- Is it realistic to expect your parent to see your hurt and try to make amends?

- Can your parent admit mistakes or accept his errors? If not, how realistic is it to point these out or to try to correct his misperceptions?

- Have you ever experienced empathy from your parent, and why do you expect it now?

All of these thoughts exhibit the yearning you have for the fantasized loving and empathic parent. Your longings are keeping the fantasy alive, contributing to your distress, and preventing you from mobilizing your resources to remain centered and grounded. These untapped inner resources could prevent you from being hurt any further.

In this chapter we looked at some common situations with self-absorbed parents that can be stressful and produce considerable discomfort. You learned strategies that can help reduce or eliminate some negative effects that these situations can produce. The next chapter describes some hidden and toxic results of your relationship with your self-absorbed parent and presents a process for strengthening your self to heal old wounds and to fortify your self against future assaults and hurts.

CHAPTER 5

Overcome the Hidden and Toxic Effects of Your Parent

Even though you may have forgotten some injuries to your self caused by your parent, repressed or denied some, or refused to think about them, they can still exert hidden and disguised effects that are toxic. What are usually undermined are your self-confidence, self-efficacy, and self-perception, all of which can have negative effects on you and your relationships. A significant part of building your self will be to detoxify.

Previous chapters have discussed how wounding occurs, how the initial wound can continue to fester, and how you can be rewounded. All of these processes produce toxic buildup. Toxic buildup refers to self-defeating behaviors and attitudes, emotional susceptibility, and destructive relationships. You don't know or understand why you continue to do these things, efforts to change have not been successful, and you are frustrated and confused about what to do that would be helpful. At this point you may be more aware of how some of your family-of-origin experiences and other past events produced your initial wounding. You may also be aware of how your personal characteristics, beliefs about yourself, and insufficient boundary strength prevent you from defending yourself against wounding, and how these contribute to the inability to heal and grow. This awareness and understanding is helpful and may even help you see where you can make constructive changes.

We now turn to discussing other possible effects on you that you may not even realize are affecting you. First, go ahead and rate yourself on the following scale:

Level of Toxicity Scale

5—Extremely descriptive of you

4—Very descriptive of you

3—Somewhat descriptive of you

2—A little descriptive of you

1—Not at all descriptive of you

In general, how often/much do you experience the following effects?

1. High to extremely high stress level   5 4 3 2 1

2. Easily irritated and cranky   5 4 3 2 1

3. Disturbed sleep, such as disquieting dreams or insomnia   5 4 3 2 1

4. Out of sorts, off balance   5 4 3 2 1

5. Distracted, lack of focus and concentration   5 4 3 2 1

6. Deflated level of enjoyment   5 4 3 2 1

7. Intrusive thoughts   5 4 3 2 1

8. Very disorganized   5 4 3 2 1

9. Dissatisfaction with your physical self   5 4 3 2 1

10. Dissatisfaction with your relationships   5 4 3 2 1

11. Dissatisfaction with your life's meaning and purpose   5 4 3 2 1

12. Dissatisfaction with your accomplishments   5 4 3 2 1

Scoring: Add your ratings to get a total score. Scores of 51 to 60 indicate a very high level of toxicity; 41 to 50 indicate a high level; 31 to 40 indicate a moderate level; 21 to 30 indicate that there is some toxicity; and scores of 20 or below indicate little or no toxicity.

There are other symptoms of possible toxicity, such as the following:

- Overeating

- Undereating

- Substance abuse

- Addictions, such as gambling and shopping

- Abusive relationships

- Depression

- Suicidal thoughts

Your wounded self is unable to heal or to protect itself. Toxic buildup can affect all aspects of your being and of your life. The rest of this chapter will focus on understanding how your behavior and attitudes can be reflective of some toxicity and providing suggestions for detoxification.

SELF-DESTRUCTIVE RESPONSES TO TOXICITY

There are many ways to handle the toxicity within you that has built up over the years, but some of the most commonly used tend to only add to your distress, or at best provide surface, momentary relief. Then, too, you may not be aware that your self-destructive behaviors are an unconscious attempt to handle your toxicity—that is, you're acting on an unconscious level. Some of these behaviors and attitudes can actually be destructive to your self-esteem and to your relationships.

As you read the descriptions for these, try to assess how much you use the particular behavior or attitude, and stay open to the possibility that you may be doing this without conscious awareness. Conscious and unconscious behaviors and attitudes that can be ineffective ways of handling toxic buildup include defense mechanisms, acts against yourself, and acts against others. Many of these are listed next, with extended explanations for each. Each section offers a reflection that will help you assess how this strategy operates in your life.

Defense Mechanisms

- Displacement

- Repression

- Denial

- Withdrawal

- Projection

Acts Against Self

- Self-blame

- Despair

- Hopelessness

- Helplessness

- Devaluing the self

Acts Against Others

- Blaming

- Acting out

- Taking advantage

- Making unreasonable demands

- Devaluing and demeaning

Defense Mechanisms

These are unconscious mechanisms for protecting the self. The five listed here are not all the defenses that can be used, but these can serve as good examples. Although they are unconscious, you can recognize them in retrospect, become more aware of your tendency to use them, and start to analyze what you are protecting yourself against. In other words, you can learn to better evaluate threats and dangers to your self, and thereby reduce your tendencies to employ your defenses. You may find that you are protecting yourself from a nonexistent threat.

DISPLACEMENT

Displacement is often used when you cannot directly attack a particular target (for instance, your parent with Destructive Narcissistic Pattern). Instead of retaliating against the offending person or absorbing the blame yourself, you find another, safer person to blame. Other family members are often the targets of choice. You've probably heard the old chestnut of someone responding to getting yelled at by the boss by going home and yelling at her spouse for some trifling error (or even an imagined one). That's displacement. It was not safe to attack the boss, and so the anger got displaced on the spouse.

REFLECTION: Think about an incident when you were unfairly accused, treated disrespectfully, or ignored and did not feel safe enough (or entitled) to protest or complain about the treatment. Now, reflect on what you did with your feelings about your treatment. Is it possible that you later displaced them on someone else?

REPRESSION

Repression is a defense mechanism where you push offending material so deep into your unconscious that no amount of effort can make you bring it to the surface. It will be difficult for you to recognize that you are using repression, and you will have to suspend disbelief for a while and accept that you most likely have engaged in this tactic. Accepting this is not difficult, as everyone has forgotten something only to remember it at a later time. That is an example of repression.

When something is repressed, the incident is buried so deeply that conscious thought cannot access it or cannot access many of the details. What happened could be so personally threatening that you want to make sure that you don't have to be aware of it. No amount of thinking, reflecting, or someone telling you about it can make you recall it. However, just because it is buried doesn't mean that it doesn't continue to affect you in numerous ways, as its influence is also on an unconscious level. For example, dislike for someone that you cannot explain could be because of some repressed material, either about that person, about a similar situation, or even about someone from your past.

REFLECTION: A common situation that can illustrate repression is when someone recalls an event and you do not recall that event, although there is evidence that you were present and should be able to recall it. Reflect on one time when this happened to you and examine if it is possible that the described event did happen, you were negatively affected, and you chose to repress it. You may still not remember it, but that doesn't mean that it didn't happen, it just means that you repressed it for your own reasons.

DENIAL

Denial is an unconscious mechanism that protects you from unacceptable and unpleasant truths about yourself. It is a deep-seated and unconscious refusal to acknowledge an event or fact that is perceived as threatening. Denial is a defense against knowing something about your self, and repression is not recalling an event that was threatening to your self. This form of denial is inaccessible to you. Your self has decided that it is much too dangerous to its continued survival for you to be aware of and accept whatever is hidden.

Much of the treatment around addictions refers to denial, and this provides a good example (although denial is used as a defense for everything and by everyone). What happens is that the addicted person cannot accept that her behavior is out of control, and that it is destructive to the person and/or to her relationships. It is much too threatening for the person to admit that she cannot do what others are able to do—recognize the compulsive and impulsive nature of the behavior and stop at a certain point. The addict will argue that she can control it at any time she chooses to, but the fact that she hasn't yet been able to exert this control belies her claim. No amount of telling, selling, insisting, or browbeating can get through to her because it is too threatening to the self to admit this weakness, lack of control, and shame. Thus she continue her denial.

REFLECTION: Are there sectors of your life where you are in denial? For example, are you in an abusive relationship, eating too much or too little, refusing to take needed medicine or to seek medical help, putting off seeing a mental health professional for your depression, overspending to gain attention and admiration, or committing illegal acts? These are some behaviors, along with addiction, that commonly result in denial.

WITHDRAWAL

Withdrawal can be both conscious and unconscious. In both cases it is a defense mechanism that takes the form of an emotional or psychological flight from present danger. While physical withdrawal does happen and is usually a conscious act, psychological and emotional withdrawal are more likely to be on a nonconscious or unconscious level.

Unconscious withdrawal causes you to be inaccessible to other people. Although you may be physically present and even interacting with others, your spirit—the real you—is hidden. When you withdraw, you put your true self elsewhere in an effort to protect it from perceived threat. Others, especially those who know you well, may sense this withdrawal, but you can remain unaware of what you are doing. Some signs of withdrawal are a wandering mind, daydreaming, mentally planning for a future act, returning to a past event, and so on.

What can be helpful for you when you recognize or become aware that you are withdrawing is to try to recall what was happening when you phased out. There was something going on in your environment that signaled that your self was threatened in some way, and so you took flight. That something was shaming, guilt producing, overwhelming, revealing of your inadequacies, and so on. You felt powerless to control and manage whatever was triggered for you, and you just decided to leave.

> REFLECTION: Try to remember a situation or event
> where you withdrew emotionally and think about what
> seemed dngerous to you at that particular moment. Use this
> information to reflect on whether this kind of perceived danger is
> what triggers withdrawal for you in other situations.

PROJECTION

We discussed projection in an earlier chapter, defining it as a person being unable to accept something about herself and then moving unconsciously to project it onto another person. The next step is when the person doing the projecting then reacts to the receiver of the projection as though she, in fact, had this unacceptable quality, feeling, or behavior. This is another way that your self can be protected from an unpleasant awareness.

Your shame, guilt, inadequacies, fears, and other negative, upsetting, and dangerous aspects of your self can be managed by (figuratively) putting them onto or in another person. You then have verification for how you respond to that person, as she now seems to you to have the unacceptable characteristic, attitude, or whatever you cannot admit to yourself that you have. You don't accept it in yourself, and you cannot accept it in the other person.

Thus your projections can negatively affect your perceptions of others, promote mistrust, and erode relationships of all kinds. Your view of reality is distorted, even if that distortion is slight, and you remain unaware of what you are doing. The other person is usually unaware that she is the recipient of your projections and does not understand your reactions. Some people are knowledgeable about projecting, but most people will never consider that possibility.

REFLECTION: Think about a situation where you had a strong negative reaction to what someone said, did, or seemed to be. Ask yourself if part or all of your reaction was based on your projection. That is, if you reacted to what seemed to be anger in the other person, could that have happened because you projected your anger onto that person so that you would not have to experience it?

Alternatives

Consider making some of the following behavior and attitude changes.

Defense Used	Change To
Displacement	Accept yourself; resist taking your dissatisfaction out on others
Repression	Work it out and resolve it with a competent therapist
Denial	Work to tolerate both positive and negative aspects of self; accept your imperfections and work to develop strengths

| Withdrawal | Develop a greater tolerance for discomfort, both yours and others; use empathic listening and responding |
| Projection | Build an awareness of when you may be projecting, and learn from this what you find unacceptable about yourself |

Acts Against Self

These are hurtful and/or destructive things you do to yourself. Others do not do or cause these; you instigate them and carry them out. And though they result in a negative outcome for you, you remain unaware of how you are contributing to your own distress. You've unconsciously internalized and incorporated your parent's negative perceptions into yourself, and you're acting to validate these as if they are true. You have accepted the negative perceptions and use many ways to ensure that these do come true. The acts discussed here are self-blame, despair, hopelessness, helplessness, and devaluing your self.

SELF-BLAME

Self-blame is not always destructive, even though it hurts. You blame yourself for your failures to live up to your expectations for yourself. This sounds okay on the surface, but it can be destructive when your expectations are unrealistic. Some examples of this sort of expectation are demanding personal perfection, feeling responsible for others' comfort, or the unexamined acceptance of the values held by those around you (by your parents, your culture, and so on).

It is hurtful enough when you can't meet your realistic expectations, but you can take comfort in the fact that you can work to change these and to do better next time. Any unrealistic expectations you have will continue to exert negative effects on you. The only help is to become more realistic about yourself, your abilities, your responsibilities, and your expectations.

REFLECTION: How often do you blame yourself for things over which you have no control? Can you remember to stop the blame and vow to do better next time? Can you applaud your successes or even recognize them? You betcha.

DESPAIR

Despair is very much like depression but may not have the physical cause that depression can, such as a neurological condition or the usual depression that accompanies recovering from a traumatic event or illness. Despair is a deflated spirit, where your inability to have things go your way is very upsetting to you. It can result when you are unable to manage and control your self, your environment, and/or your relationships over a period of time, and you fear that things will never get better for you.

Your sense of self-efficacy is determined in large part by your ability to get your needs met. Now, this doesn't say anything about the reasonableness, logic, and rationality of your needs. It only speaks to your getting them met. In fact, your needs can be reasonable or unreasonable, logical or illogical, rational or irrational, and can still be met or not met. What seems to be important is that you believe you have enough ability and influence to get them met. That's what self-efficacy means.

Despair can result when you believe that you cannot act or have someone else act to meet your needs. Despair will not allow you to do any of the positive acts in this list:

■ Perceive when you are influential and effective

■ Be optimistic about yourself and the future

■ Bounce back from disappointments and other negative life events

■ See and appreciate positive aspects of your self, your existence, or your relationships

■ Obtain enjoyment from life

If this description fits you, the suggestions on creativity and inspiration in chapter 9 can be helpful.

REFLECTION: Is it possible that you are despairing when the reality is very different? Are you realistic about your ability to influence and control events, or are your expectations reflective of some untamed grandiosity, where you think you should be more powerful and have more control than is realistic or reasonable?

HOPELESSNESS

Closely aligned with despair is hopelessness, which is defined here as an inability to imagine that things can even be better or improve. It is not so much a deflation of the spirit as it is a lack of visualization, imagination, realistic wishing, and knowledge. You cannot see your way out, how to fix the situation, or that you will be rescued. There is no hope.

This lack of hope can contribute to depression and despair. Studies on the mind-body connection point to the negative physical effects of hopelessness (Hafen et al 1996). You can really contribute to your own physical, emotional, spiritual, and relational lack of well-being when you lack hope.

There are situations where it is almost impossible to foster and maintain hope. In his book *Man's Search for Meaning*, Viktor Frankl describes his internment in the German labor camps during World War II, a situation that many felt was without hope. There are other such situations, such as a terminal illness, death of a loved one, being convicted of a crime, or diagnosis of a chronic condition, among others. No amount of hope will change these circumstances, and it is unrealistic to hold out false hope. However, even in these situations hopelessness is not inevitable. There are always other aspects of your self and your life that hold the potential for hope. You may not be able to change your circumstances, but you do have some influence and control over how you *react* to them. You also have a responsibility to take care of yourself as best you can, and being hopeless is not helpful to your self-care.

REFLECTION: What have you given up on and become hopeless about? What may you be missing because of your hopelessness? What can you do to be more hopeful in other parts of your life?

HELPLESSNESS

Helplessness is discussed separate from hopelessness because it has more negative connotations for self-perception than does hopelessness. Lack of hope carries with it an implication that there are some outside influences that are preventing the person from being effective, whereas helplessness is totally within the person. This person, at this time, does not have the wherewithal to be effective. Thus, helplessness is seen as a personal inadequacy and as failure.

Some examples for helplessness can include feeling, saying, or doing the following:

- Not knowing what to do or say

- Seeing an injustice or unfair act but not being able to stop it

- Perceiving that you or someone else is on a self-destructive path and feeling unable to successfully intervene

- Unable to prevent abusive acts toward yourself

- Disappointing yourself or someone else

- Feeling someone's pain but remaining unable to fix it

- Repeating the same mistake, such as choosing intimate partners who betray you

All these examples are focused on you and your inability to be effective, for if you were different, better, good enough, less flawed, and so on, you would not have to experience feeling or being helpless. At least that's what you probably tell yourself. What you're overlooking or ignoring is that no one can be perfectly competent all of the time, and that feeling helpless is a signal or indication of where you need more personal development, better skills, a deeper understanding, or a more realistic appraisal of your abilities and expectations for yourself.

Responses to feeling helpless fall into one of five categories: give up, leave, persist, blame outside factors, and building the self. Giving up and letting events take their course can be a response that either mires you deeper in your sense of helplessness or is a realistic appraisal of the situation. Leaving is a form of withdrawing to protect yourself from having to confront your helplessness. Persisting in trying to be effective can either be a continuation of what you were doing that was ineffective, or it could bear positive results. It's really amazing how often all of us continue to do something that does not work, did not work, and will not work, but still we persist. Blaming outside factors for your helplessness is a common response and is seen when we begin to rationalize a situation (a common defense against feeling helpless). It is also possible that outside factors are indeed a barrier or constraint. The most positive response is to build your self, so that when you feel helpless you can be assured that either you're overlooking a personal resource that could assist you, or that there truly is nothing you can do.

REFLECTION: What is your response to feeling helpless? How can you recognize your underused personal resources? Can you think of ways to use your identified resources to be more effective? Are you being realistic about yourself and the situation when you experience helplessness? Are you looking for someone to rescue you?

DEVALUING THE SELF

Devaluing yourself is a particularly destructive response to toxic buildup. The world confronts you every day with your inadequacies, ineffectiveness, lack of ability, and other negative possibilities. When you add to these inevitable challenges a refusal to appreciate your positive qualities, you end up only increasing the negative effects on yourself.

The roots of your devaluation of yourself are located in your early family-of-origin experiences and other past experiences. Your self-perception is most heavily influenced in its development by the reactions to you by others in your environment—that is, your family and other significant people in your world. You may have internalized some negative self-perceptions you incorporated from your parent early on, and these led you to devalue yourself. You may even have a habit of focusing more on what you perceive to be negative personal qualities than your positive ones.

Devaluing is not a form of modesty, being self-effacing, or shunning the limelight. It is much more negative than these, and if you give any of these as an excuse, you are fooling yourself. You can be any or all of these without devaluing yourself.

REFLECTION: How can you become more aware of devaluing yourself, either to others or to yourself? How often do you minimize your achievements, the things that you do well and like about yourself? Are you afraid of being thought of as arrogant, boasting, bragging, or the like? How can you develop a more realistic view of your strengths and other positive qualities so that you can better appreciate them?

OVERVALUING THE SELF

Overvaluing yourself can also result from toxic buildup, where you protect yourself from shame and feeling inadequate by inflating your characteristics, actions, and accomplishments. In this instance, boasting, bragging, and playing one-upmanship are common behaviors and attitudes. Cutthroat competition, jealousy and envy, power struggles, and other negative reactions hurt you, others, and your relationships. All these can be the outcomes of perceiving a strong need to protect yourself.

Some behaviors and attitudes that can be a reflection of over-valuing include the following:

- Never admitting mistakes or errors

- Feeling that you would not make errors if others did what they were supposed to do

- Thinking that your contributions are of more importance than others'

- Failing to accept personal responsibility

- Defending, rationalizing, or minimizing your negative attributes

- Feeling jealousy and envy toward others

- Feeling superior to and contempt for others

- Feeling entitled to special treatment

- Seeking admiration and attention

- Continually boasting and bragging about your accomplishments and/or possessions

These behaviors and attitudes are associated with underdeveloped narcissism and fears of abandonment and destruction. The inability to understand and accept that others are also worthwhile and unique, together with the need to protect the self from imagined dangers, leads to self-absorption that negatively affects your relationships and prevents growth and development for those parts of your self that need them.

REFLECTION: Are any or most of these behaviors and attitudes reflective of you? Have you been criticized for any of these? Could it be that you cannot see these behaviors and attitudes as reflective of yourself? Are you refusing to see or admit that some of these are descriptive of you?

Alternatives

Now that I've described some toxic behaviors, attitudes, and acts against the self, I'll describe some positive changes you can make for each. The reflections probably gave you some ideas about how you are responding to the toxic buildup and how you are defending against knowing this about your self.

Consider making some of the following changes.

Current Behavior/Attitude	Change To
Self-blame	Realize and accept reasonable limits on your personal responsibility.
Despair	Realisticaly appraise of your personal power and efficacy, and when external events and situations are beyond your control.
Hopelessness	Develop a vision for some realistic possibilities and work to achieve these.
Helplessness	Become more independent and do more for yourself, depending less on others.
Devaluing yourself	Accept both your weaknesses and your strengths; build on your strengths.
Overvaluing yourself	Become more realistic and balanced about your perceptions of your capabilities, talents, and so on.

Acts Against Others

The third category for possible hidden toxic effects is acts against others, the things you do or say that are unconsciously designed to off-load your feelings of shame, guilt, inadequacy, and fear. As may be obvious, these behaviors are destructive to relationships, do not succeed in getting rid of your unwanted feelings and perceptions about yourself, and aren't helpful in your constructive personal development. Acts against others include blaming, acting out, taking advantage, making unreasonable demands, and using devaluing and demeaning remarks, such as sarcasm and put-downs.

BLAMING

Blaming others for their mistakes or inadequacies, or to keep you from admitting your responsibility, is a common response to toxic buildup. It is much easier to see other people's faults, flaws, and errors than it is to see your own. It is also easier to point these out in the hope that you will not have to take any responsibility for whatever went awry. Further, blaming others is a way to show your superiority and their inferiority.

Yes, others do make mistakes, can be inadequate, and so on. No one is disputing that. However, your tendency to blame others goes beyond noticing these faults, flaws, and errors. You are trying to shame the blamed person and to make her feel guilty. Just think of how you feel when you are blamed—either justly or unfairly. You feel shame for not being good enough, guilty for not living up to your standards, anger that the other person pointed this out, and fear that, because you were found wanting, you will be abandoned or destroyed. Now, you may say that you don't feel this intensely, but you are most likely to feel some of each emotion. The person you blame will have similar feelings and reactions. Even if the person actually *is* to blame, your pointing it out does not help the relationship or the situation.

Your tendency to blame others can be a result of your family-of-origin experiences, and other past experiences where you observed others who were blaming. You may consciously or unconsciously be choosing to imitate this behavior. Some people who are blaming are projecting their personal feelings of shame and the like. So, it becomes more difficult for you to know why you are blaming. It can be helpful for you to realize that blaming is neither constructive nor helpful in many circumstances.

> *REFLECTION: How often do you verbally or nonverbally try to blame others? Can you become more aware of when you want to blame and then refrain from doing so?*

ACTING OUT

"Acting out" is a term used in therapy to cover a variety of defiant, oppositional, disruptive, and other distressing behaviors. An example of acting out is when you interrupt an existing conversation and change the topic so that you can take over, become the focus of attention, and trigger some feelings in the people you interrupted. The following story is another example.

An experienced high school teacher was taking a class at a local university to update her teaching certificate. As she reported later to her sister, she behaved uncharacteristically and badly in the class, chewing bubble gum and blowing bubbles and even giving the instructor another student's name as her own. She seldom chewed gum of any kind and did not allow chewing gum in her high school classes. She told her sister that she could not imagine why she behaved as she did. Her sister asked her how she felt about the class, and she responded that she was disgruntled about having to give up her free time to take it. The subject and the teacher were okay, but she felt angry that she was required to take the class. Her resulting behavior was a vivid acting out of her resentment about what she felt was a lack of control over the use of her time. She also reported that she had apologized to the teacher after class.

There are numerous ways to act out that irritate and annoy but may not be serious enough for anyone to bring them to your attention. The following are some examples:

- Breaking or ignoring minor rules

- Failing to follow directions or guidelines

- Talking when someone else is talking

- Sulking, withdrawing, and the like

- Indirectly attacking or putting others down

- Refusing to cooperate

- Forgetting to do something you promised to do

- Retaliating for real or imagined slights, betrayals, or rejection

- Refusing to consider alternatives and insisting on getting your way at all times

Instead of respectful, cooperative mutuality and interdependence, acting-out behavior signals the opposite.

REFLECTION: Could some of your behaviors be acting out? You need to become more aware of the possibility that you are being resistant, defiant, and oppositional at times and work to understand what triggers these responses for you.

TAKING ADVANTAGE

Taking advantage refers to exploitation of others for your gain. You, perhaps unconsciously, have a need to show your superiority, power, control, or manipulative ability and do so at the expense of the other person. Taking advantage demonstrates your contempt for that person, thinking that she is weak, unworthy, and of lesser value.

You may think that you never take advantage of others in this way, and indeed you may not. But if you do any of the following, you are taking advantage:

- Cutting in line

- Not merging early when a road lane is closed

- Ordering a child to do something for you that you could do for yourself, such as fetch something

- Entering someone's room or office without knocking

- Making plans, social engagements, and the like without consulting with your spouse, partner, or other affected family members

- Shaming others or trying to promote their guilt to get your way or to have them do what you want them to do

- Getting a subordinate to do part of your work, personal things, or extra work for no pay or credit

- Putting your name on reports and the like when you had little or no contribution to their development

- Taking what others have, or what they give you, with no reciprocity

- Expecting to receive preferential treatment

Exploitation is a behavior and characteristic of underdeveloped narcissism where the person has not yet developed an acceptance and tolerance for other people as worthwhile and unique. Rather, she thinks of others as extensions of herself and thus under her control. It can also be a result of toxic buildup, where you are avenging your hurts on others and shoring up your self-perception by undermining other people.

REFLECTION: If you take advantage of others, do you want to continue this behavior? How can you become more aware of when you do this, and what do you need to do to stop doing it?

MAKING UNREASONABLE DEMANDS

Most people believe that the demands they make on others are reasonable. You would not make them otherwise. But you need to suspend judgment for a little while and take a good look at what you demand from others, how you communicate these demands, how you react when they are met or not met, and the impact of these on others and on your relationships.

What demands are unreasonable? Although you may think that you are making requests, verbalizing your wants and needs, pointing out needed behavioral changes and attitude changes others should make, and trying to make things better, you are more likely to be demanding that these be done in accord with what you think. Demands are unreasonable when they require any or all of the following:

- Another person to change because you want them to change

- Other people to read your mind and give you what you want, desire, or need

- Others to give you attention and/or admiration

- Preferential treatment for you

- Others, such as your children, ordering their lives as you want them to

- Others to maintain their dependency on you

These unreasonable demands are intended to order and control your world, and this need of yours could be a hidden or masked response to your toxic buildup. When other people don't meet your demands, ignore them, or consider them unreasonable, you encounter more toxic buildup. In this way, you continually reinforce some unconscious self-perceptions about your efficacy and worth.

REFLECTION: How can you become more independent? Can you try to think of others as independent to do or not do what they want to, just as you want this for yourself? What can you do to reduce or eliminate what may be my unreasonable demands?

DEVALUING AND DEMEANING

Just as with some other behaviors and attitudes we've previously examined, devaluing and demeaning remarks and actions are intended to demonstrate your superiority, power, and control. These remarks and actions are used to show the other person as inferior, flawed, shamed, of lesser value, inept, and so on, and that you are none of these. Sometimes these are offered under the guise of being helpful to that person, there is an attempt to disguise them with humor, or they are presented as if that person doesn't know any better and you are rescuing her. These are rationalizations you may use to convince yourself that you are not really harming the other person.

Motives for such remarks or actions include projection and revenge. As we've seen, projection happens when you take something unacceptable in you and put it on or in the other person so that you can openly reject that something. Thus, you don't have to deal with your awareness of that unacceptable part of yourself and can let everyone around you know that you don't like whatever it is by your devaluing and/or demeaning remarks. Revenge can also be an unconscious motive, where you are attacking someone else because of hurts you received earlier in your life.

There are no positive reasons or outcomes for devaluing and demeaning remarks and actions. They don't foster development of a positive relationship, and they don't endear you to the target of your remarks or to anyone who observes them. People around you are more likely to have sympathy for your target and to think less of you. Try to become aware of and stop using any of the following:

- Sarcastic remarks and comments

- Put-downs

- Jokes at another person's expense

- Deliberately misleading or misinforming someone

- Making critical comments either to a person's face or behind her back

- Criticizing whatever you find objectionable, such as a person's clothes, body, hair, or possessions

- Suggesting that someone is incompetent, inept, and the like

- Constantly or even infrequently confronting people with stories of their mistakes and the like

- Failing to show respect

- Ignoring or overlooking others

REFLECTION: Do you consciously or unconsciously demean or devalue some people at times? How do you deal with your need to feel superior, powerful, and in control when you are with others? Is your self so needy or weak that you must devalue others in order to feel adequate or superior?

Alternatives

Acts against others can have negative effects on relationships. You can begin to build more satisfying relationships with the following suggested changes.

From Negative	To Positive
Blaming	Regardless of what happens, accept that blame does not help in any way.

Acting out	Become aware of when you are acting out, reflect on your reasons, and stop.
Taking advantage	Recognize and accept others as separate from you and as being entitled to respect. Give up trying to manipulate others.
Making unreasonable demands	Develop a greater awareness of your entitlement attitude, cultivate respect for the rights and responsibilities of others, and reflect on what it is that you really want.
Devaluing and demeaning	Cease sarcastic and other devaluing remarks; explore your need for superiority, power, and control; and have a greater appreciation for others as unique and worthwhile individuals.

DETOXIFYING YOURSELF

You most likely found one or more ways that you could be exhibiting results of hidden toxic buildup and some strategies for overcoming these. The next two chapters focus on strategies for detoxifying your self, building your self with strong and resilient boundaries, and letting go of the negative experiences and feelings that formed the toxic material. We've begun the process by helping you to become more aware of the toxic effects of your Destructive Narcissistic Parent, and your self-defeating acts both the obvious ones and the more elusive ones.

To change any or all of these responses to toxic buildup requires thought, self-awareness, time, and effort. They took some time to insinuate their effects in and on your life, and it will take time to change them. Be patient with yourself, forgive lapses and errors, resolve to do better next time, and stay in touch with and be pleased about your positive accomplishments.

The previous chart gives you some possible target behavior and attitude changes you can make. Don't try to do all of these at once. Select one or two to work on, and when you feel you've made progress, select another one or two. This will help you concentrate on your goal without overwhelming you. It can be discouraging to take on too much at one time, and I don't want you to become discouraged and stop trying.

CHAPTER 6

Eight Strategies to Stop Hurting

The most constructive and enduring strategy for lessening or eliminating negative effects of the self-absorbed parent on you is to develop a stronger and more resilient self. This not only allows you to have better interactions with that parent but also enhances your other relationships to make them more meaningful, satisfying, and long lasting. Adopting constructive strategies is more rewarding in the long run than continuing to try to get your parent to change, as the effort you put into changing him is unlikely to be successful. Turn your time, effort, and emotional investment to developing yourself.

In the rest of the book we'll be focusing on information and strategies you can use to build a self that is hardy, strong, resilient, and capable of initiating and maintaining meaningful and satisfying relationships, a self that does not continue to suffer the ill effects of a self-absorbed parent. The eight strategies we'll be looking at are:

1. Giving up the fantasy

2. Using self-talk and positive affirmations

3. Performing altruistic acts

4. Reaching out to others

5. Finding beauty and wonder

6. Changing the pace

7. Bringing mindfulness into your life

8. Eliminating personal self-absorbed behaviors and attitudes

These strategies are related to building a stronger and more independent self. This fortified "you" will help you protect yourself from wounding by things your parent says and does, will help to heal old hurts so that you can view them more objectively from your stronger and better-protected self, and will allow you to let go of negative feelings associated with old wounds. In addition, this stronger self will gradually detoxify so that you can reduce or eliminate most of the defenses, acts against self, and acts against others. You will also be able to work to develop meaningful relationships, and to be more successful at coping with your self-absorbed parent.

But before we move on, let's assess where you are in terms of letting go of negative feelings and overcoming toxicity.

Exercise 6.1: Level of Overcoming Toxicity

Materials: Several sheets of paper and a pen or pencil for writing

Procedure:

1. Sit in silence and reflect on the course of your life, noting both the positive and negative events.

2. When you are ready, open your eyes and list eight to ten wounding events, comments, and the like that you remember your destructive narcissistic parent doing.

3. List your feelings about each event separately and then give each feeling an intensity rating from 0 (no intensity) to 10 (extreme intensity).

4. Review and reassess each event separately. You can do this more effectively by doing the following steps in order:

    a. Close your eyes.

    b. Recall the event and your emotions.

c. Check how you feel now about the event as you are doing this part of the exercise.

d. Open your eyes and revise the rating if it's changed—either higher or lower.

e. Put a line through all that have an emotional intensity rating of 0. You have let go of these.

5. Use a clean sheet of paper and write a new list of the revised events that have emotional intensity ratings of 5 or above. Keep this list, as we will work with it in the last chapter.

It is possible that some event you reviewed no longer carries the high level of emotional intensity it did when you first listed it. You have moved on, not forgetting or forgiving, but you don't hurt now as much as you did then. This is progress, even if the intensity rating has decreased only one level. In addition, you've probably shed some resentments, grudges, and so on as you've worked through these chapters and gained more awareness and understanding. Take a moment to celebrate your progress, even if it was only one event you feel differently about. Look at how far you've come, not how far you have to go.

Exercise 6.2: Celebrate Progress

1. Take inventory of how your body and emotions feel now that you are not carrying that baggage. Also, celebrate events where the emotional intensity has lessened. That, too, is progress and should be applauded. Knowing that progress is being made, albeit slowly, can be a great motivator.

2. Do something tangible to celebrate your progress. For example, you can draw a picture, construct a collage, jump up and down, release a balloon, get a flower and display it in a pretty vase, dance around to a favorite piece of music (or to no music at all), or skip around and smile.

LETTING GO OF FANTASY

Let's turn to some constructive things you can do to handle your toxic buildup. The first strategy is something that is difficult to do, because it involves awareness of a fantasy you did not know you had. That is, you have a fantasy about your wounding events and your self-absorbed parent. Many fantasies have one or more of the following scenarios:

- Your parent admits his errors and the way he has hurt you and makes amends.

- Your parent suffers because of what was done to you.

- You are able to outperform your parent and can rub his nose in your superiority.

- Everyone around him sees him as you do and rejects him.

- You are vindicated.

- You are able to do to your parent what he did to you, or someone else does that to the parent.

- Your parent will change and regret what he did or said.

These fantasies are helping your negative feelings persist, and they reinforce these bad feelings. They are fantasies because they are unlikely to happen just because you wish they would. Neither your parent nor anyone else is going to change because you want them to. Your parent probably perceives events and situations differently than you do, or he is unaware of or insensitive to your wounding. Your wishes, dreams, and fantasies about your self-absorbed parent are not helpful at all.

How do you know if you are carrying one or more fantasies? Assess yourself on the items below using the following ratings.

Your Fantasies Scale

5—You very intensely want this to happen.

4—You intensely want this to happen.

3—You would be pleased if this happened but don't often think about it.

2—You are ambivalent about this happening.

1—You do not want this to happen.

Directions: Think of your self-absorbed parent and rate the extent to which you wish and yearn for the described event in each item.

1. Your parent would admit he was wrong and say that he is sorry.   5 4 3 2 1

2. Your parent would hug you and tell you that you are wonderful.   5 4 3 2 1

3. Your parent would get out of your life and you would never have to see him again.   5 4 3 2 1

4. Other people would perceive your self-absorbed parent as you do and would be disapproving.   5 4 3 2 1

5. Your parent would start to realize what he has done that was so hurtful to you, regret it, and feel ashamed   5 4 3 2 1.

6. You would get even in a spectacular way.   5 4 3 2 1

Scoring: Add your ratings to derive a total score. Scores of 26 to 30 indicate that you have intense fantasies; 20 to 25 indicate numerous but less intense fantasies; 13 to 19 indicate many fantasies, off and on; 6 to 12 indicate some fantasies with some moderate intensity; and 0 to 5 indicate few such fantasies.

These fantasies result as reactions to your wounding and can have varying levels and intensities depending on the deepness of the wound to your self. The stronger reactions are usually found for the deepest hurt. You may want revenge, validation for your hurt feelings, and some signs that your parent loves you. Your feelings are powerful and can contribute to the hurt you carry because you are longing for something that will not happen, or is unlikely to happen. Those fantasies with ratings of 3 or higher are keeping you mired and stuck instead of letting you grow and develop. Logically you know that your parent will not change, but you keep hoping for that, feeling that this is what you need to heal. The reality is something different, and you can heal without the parent having to change. A step to healing is to relinquish these fantasies, or to reduce them to so low an intensity that you can easily dismiss them when they emerge.

Strategies to Reduce Fantasies and Become More Realistic

Awareness of your fantasies is the first step. But how do you stop having them? That's not as easy to do. You have to work through and resolve your feelings about the injury and the person to accomplish this completely. But one strategy that can help begin the process is for you to engage in some self-talk in your thoughts every time you begin to be aware of the fantasies, wishes, and desires about your parent or a particular event. For example, if you were wishing that your parent would see the error of his ways and change, some self-talk statements to help would include the following:

- It is unrealistic to expect that he will change, and wishing won't make it happen.

- I cannot change another person.

- I will rise above this.

- I need to accept my parent as he is and not expect him to meet my expectations.

- Nothing has worked to this point, so why am I expecting it to work now?

- I don't need to hurt my parent in order to feel better.

- I'll love, accept, and approve of myself.

- I've got more constructive and satisfying things to do than this.

Continue to work on giving up your fantasies, as this will not happen just because you think you have decided to give them up; they tend to persist in your nonconscious and unconscious, lurking undetected. Try not to become impatient with yourself when you find that you still have some fantasies—they're tough to get rid of. Just say to yourself that you have more work to do, the hurt was deeper than you thought, and you will overcome at some point.

Now let's turn to some self-building strategies that will also reduce your need for these fantasies.

SELF-STATEMENTS AND SELF-AFFIRMATIONS

Your self-absorbed parent is probably adept at triggering your insecurities, negative thoughts about your self, feelings of inadequacy, and so on. A contributor to the trigger can be what you say to yourself about you, or self-statements. It doesn't help that what you're telling yourself is probably inaccurate, unrealistic, illogical, and negative. You can short-circuit this process by realizing when your thoughts and feelings are responses to negative self-statements and substituting self-affirmations. Some possible self-affirmations to counter the usual self-statements follow. You can also develop your own self-affirmations.

Self-statement: My parent's criticism of me is correct.

Self-affirmation: I have many strengths and talents.

Self-statement: I should attend to others' demands and expectations for me, even if I think they are unrealistic.

Self-affirmation: I can decide for myself what I should do and don't have to give in to others' demands and expectations.

Self-statement: I must always meet others' expectations, even when these are too high, unrealistic, or demanding.

Self-affirmation: I do meet many expectations held by others, but I don't have to meet all of them.

Self-statement: I'm searching for external affirmation of my worth.

Self-affirmation: I can value and cherish myself without requiring external validation.

Self-statement: I'm supposed to control everything.

Self-affirmation: I am able to handle and resolve most events.

Self-statement: It's my duty to keep others from feeling distress.

Self-affirmation: I can care about others without catching their feelings, and thereby be more effective.

Self-statement: I should be perfect.

Self-affirmation: I have many strengths, and I am working on what I perceive as flaws.

Self-statement: I should never make mistakes.

Self-affirmation: I am able to learn from my mistakes.

Self-statement: If I were better, I'd have better relationships.

Self-affirmation: I'm good enough and can form meaningful relationships.

Self-statement: I'm supposed to take on others' feelings and take care of them.

Self-affirmation: My boundaries can be strong so that I can care for others without becoming enmeshed or overwhelmed. I can recognize the limits of my responsibility for others' welfare.

PURSUE ALTRUISM

Acts of altruism are gifts to others that are free from obligations, expectations, demands, reciprocity, or any strings. You give freely not because you are forced, shamed, or guilty, or for your satisfaction. You give because you want the other person to have whatever it is. Gifts can be tangible or intangible.

The few studies done on altruism have all pointed out the beneficial effects for the person who gives the gift or action. Yes, the receiver gets the gift, but the giver also receives a positive outcome—even when the receiver does not know the giver. So, you can bestow a gift without the receiver's knowledge and still receive the benefits from your altruism. The following benefits result from altruistic acts: they boost health by protecting you from stress, promote a sense of well-being, decrease problems with stress-induced illnesses, and have a direct positive link to the immune system (Karren, Hafen, Frandsen, and Smith 1996)

The saying about performing random acts of kindness suggests a way to be altruistic. These random acts offer an unexpected gift of kindness without any strings, and that is altruistic. You may think of yourself as a kind person, and you probably are. But when you are kind only when it is expected of you, or just in those instances where you expect to reap some benefit or reward, that is not altruism. In other words, you choose where to bestow your kindness. Altruism would be when you do kind acts for anyone, and you do not expect anything for yourself to result from what you do.

In order to understand altruism, let's contrast it with acts and attitudes that may be good or helpful (or not), but are not altruistic. Such acts and attitudes include the following:

- Expecting or demanding a thank-you

- Wanting or needing expressions of appreciation

- Doing something to gain attention or admiration

- Asking someone if he likes what you give him or what you did for him, demonstrating your need for approval

- Reminding someone of what you did for him or what you gave him

- Expecting something in return for what you do or for what you give

- Using gifts to manipulate or to form alliances

- Trying to buy your way into someone's affections

- Bragging or boasting to others about what you did for someone or what you gave him

- Becoming angry or upset when you feel your gift was not appreciated or not appreciated enough

As you can see these are not acts or attitudes that are free from demands, expectations, or strings. They may not be all that terrible or uncommon, but they aren't altruism.

You may wonder what you can do or say that would be altruistic. You first have to accept the idea that altruistic acts are performed without strings—they will be freely given. Second, you may need to remind yourself of this notion from time to time. Third, you will want to derive your own set of altruistic acts, but you can begin with one or more of the following:

- Volunteer work of all kinds

- Tutoring or mentoring a child

- Visiting the elderly or people with limited mobility

- Teaching a craft or the like at a community center, day care, homeless shelter, or senior center

- Collecting books for homeless children

- Giving a single mother babysitting for an afternoon out

- Cutting the grass for a sick neighbor

- Making audio tapes of books for the visually impaired

- Giving words of encouragement and support

- Expressing your appreciation

- Coming to someone's aid without having to be asked

REACH OUT TO OTHERS

When you can learn how to reach out to others without becoming enmeshed or overwhelmed or always fearing being abandoned or destroyed, you are making significant progress in building your self. Our relations and connections with others are significant support for our positive self-perceptions and good physical and emotional health, and are part of what gives meaning and purpose to our lives. Thus, there are many significant benefits of reaching out to others.

If you are reading this book, then you have had many hurtful experiences that are giving you ample reason to be wary about reaching out. After all, it's wise to learn from your experiences. You may even have pulled back so far that you often feel isolated and alienated. Finding a way to reach out to others can be helpful in reducing these feelings.

You may have to use some self-talk to get started. For example, you can remind yourself of your goal: to try not to be disappointed, and to try to understand others' responses rather than giving up when it appears that someone is not as responsive as you would like. Meaningful relationships usually take time to develop, and instant intimacy is often disappointing.

What are some possibilities for reaching out to others? Read the list provided in the section on altruism for some ideas. These can also be used as starting points for reaching out to others. But remember that using them this way would include the expectation of beneficial results, so these acts wouldn't qualify as altruism. You're still being helpful, but you are also trying to make a connection to benefit yourself.

Let's say that you initiate contact in an effort to reach out. Where do you go from there? Try some or all of the following:

- Show real interest in another person.

- Listen to another person more often than you talk about your concerns in interactions with him.

- Find something to appreciate about the person and be willing to communicate this.

- Respect others' psychological boundaries and make sure that yours are also respected.

- Don't rush to solve other people's problems or concerns. Show confidence in their ability to take care of whatever is needed.

- Don't try to take over other people's lives, and don't let yours be taken over.

- Acknowledge and respect differences of opinion, values, thoughts, and so on.

- Find mutual interests and activities.

Reaching out to others does not mean that you will never again experience wounding. You may. But if you are building your self at the same time, the wounding will be mild, and you will be more easily able to soothe, fix, or let go of it. This is part of your overall goal to heal past wounding and to minimize current and future wounding.

OPEN YOURSELF TO BEAUTY AND WONDER

Beauty cannot be defined because it is individualistic. Different people find different things to be beautiful, and what seems beautiful to one person may not seem beautiful to someone else. Wonder is also individualistic. It is the childlike quality of noticing something new and novel, being curious, and deriving excitement and interest from the world around you. It's like when a child discovers something for the first time and becomes thrilled, fascinated, and intrigued.

Beauty and wonder are discussed here because they can be enriching, and that which enriches us and our lives is constructive. The ability to appreciate beauty and feel wonder adds dimensions to our lives that expand our consciousness of our world and of our selves. This ability and openness helps us transcend or expand what is ordinary, mundane, or even depressing.

Although the perception of beauty can vary from person to person, let's focus on what you find beautiful. Try the following exercise.

Exercise 6.3: Your Perception of Beauty

Materials: Sheets of paper, a pen or pencil for writing, and a set of crayons, felt markers, or colored pencils

Procedure: Find a quiet place where you will not be disturbed or disrupted.

1. Sit in silence and think of the concept of beauty. Close your eyes if that is helpful to you.

2. Next, write down all the thoughts, ideas, things, and so on that come to mind as you think about beauty. Some items on my list include the following:

- My children and grandchildren

- Finding a good solution to a problem

- Colors

- Flowers

- Animals

- Frank Lloyd Wright's productions

- J. W. Turner's paintings

- Colorful hot air balloons

- Modern contemporary shapes

- Scandinavian furniture

- The faces of happy children

- A soft snowfall that covers lightly

Once I get started, I can go on for a long time, but you get the idea.

3. Select one item and make a list of feelings evoked in you as you focus and reflect on it.

4. On another sheet of paper, select a different color for each feeling on your list. Visualize and draw a large circle on the page, and fill in the circle with the colors in any manner you choose. That is, you can use precise shapes for the feelings you color in, abstractions such as splotches of color, and so on.

5. Review what you wrote and drew. Note the feelings aroused in you as you think about what you find beautiful. Now write a short statement, paragraph, or even a phrase, that tries to capture the essence of your perception of beauty.

Once you generate your list and definition, you will need to move to the next step: noticing the beauty around you. Make a pledge to yourself to see something of beauty every day. Doing so is another way to nourish and refresh your self. Too often you may be focused so much on things you cannot change, problems you cannot solve, and planning for the future, that you miss out on your chances to notice beauty in your world. Pay more attention and seek out the beauty that comes your way.

Another enriching experience will be to expand your concept of beauty to include new things. You may want to consider things like some of the following to determine if they could fit into your definition of beauty:

- Smiles and other pleasant facial expressions

- A summer, spring, fall, or winter day

- Scenery, such as a mountain, desert, or beach

- Children at play

- A well-constructed phrase, sentence, or book

- Music other than your favorite kind

- Moving performances, such as athletic or dramatic

The world is full of beauty; we just have to be open to seeing it.

Wonder is also all around if you have a sense of humor, curiosity, and interest, and are open to learning new things. When you look at something in a new way, it can seem different and you've learned something new about it. Wonder is a characteristic inventors, scientists, scholars, and others who invent or discover knowledge have. Children have an abundant supply, as everything they encounter for the first time is a source for wonder. This is one of the reasons that they ask so many "what" and "why" questions.

You are now an adult and you know more, have narrowed and refined your interests, have made choices on the basis of what you like and what you don't like, and most likely have restricted your sense of wonder. It can be helpful and rewarding to recapture some of the wonder you had as a child.

Exercise 6.4: Cultivating Wonder

Materials: Paper, a pen or pencil for writing, and a set of crayons, felt markers, or colored pencils

Procedure: Find a place to work where you will not be disturbed.

1. Sit in silence and recall your childhood. Select one activity, event, or thing that you remember and focus on it. You can choose whatever emerges for you, such as the following:

   ■ Skipping around the room or down the street

   ■ Hiking with your parents

   ■ Learning how to play a musical instrument

   ■ Seeing anything for the first time, such as a big animal, leaf, rock, and so on

   ■ Your first look at your just-born sibling

   ■ Your mother's or father's hair

   ■ Being in the city or in the country

   ■ Flying on an airplane for the first time

2. Once you have selected your activity or thing, focus on that and try to recall the sensations, thoughts, and feelings you had at the time. Close your eyes if that helps to put you back into the experience.

3. When you feel you have captured your earlier sensations, thoughts, and feelings, write these down on a sheet of paper. Pay particular attention to the intensity of each.

4. Use your crayons, felt markers, or pencils to draw the scene, or symbols for your sensations, thoughts, and feelings. Use light colors for intensities 0 to 3, medium colors for intensities 4 to 7, and dark colors for intensities above 7.

5. Use another sheet of paper and make a list of where and how these sensations, thoughts, and feelings are present in your current life. Make another list of where and how you can capture or recapture some or all of these in your current life.

If you find that you cannot recapture some delight, interest, or pleasure from doing some of the things you previously enjoyed, you may be depressed, as this is one of the symptoms. Although the depression may be mild or situational, it could be helpful to get medical and therapeutic assistance before it becomes deeper and more enduring.

You may feel that you are too mature to enjoy doing things you did as you grew up, or you may be physically unable to engage in childhood activities or have other constraints. This does not have to limit your search for wonder. You can develop new interests and curiosity. These come from within and are under your control. People get ideas from noticing things all around them every day. They wonder about many things and ask questions like the following:

■ How does that work?

- Why does this happen?

- How did she do that?

- What would happen if _____?

- Can I find out _____?

- What would make this better?

- What can I do that would be helpful?

- What's in this?

- Why do they do that?

If you have a sense of wonder, you can always find something of interest, you are never bored, and you continue to grow and develop in constructive ways.

CHANGE OF PACE

Routine can be comforting because it is known and consistent. You do not have to be alert, careful, or think about possibilities. People who grew up in homes that did not have these qualities can be edgy, tense, and always on guard. They may expect problems and have a variety of physical and psychological concerns. Disorganization, chaos, unpredictability, and unreliability can be very upsetting, especially if they are a part of your regular life. These can make you long for routine, consistency, and predictability so that you can rest, relax, and become calm.

However, you can also become so stuck in one or more routines that you limit yourself from expanding your horizons, meeting new people or challenges, learning and developing your resources and talents, and limiting your choices. Thus, you place constraints on yourself and limit your personal growth and development in some ways. An occasional change of pace can energize you and your thoughts in many ways, enrich your inner self, and provide for wonder and beauty in your life.

This is not to say that you should disrupt your life and do away with your routines. Some routines are beneficial. For example, I do my writing in the morning, shortly after I wake up. I first read the paper and have a cup of coffee. After that I pick up my pad and pen and begin to write. Yes, I'm still in the dark ages of writing with a pad and pen. They go almost everywhere with me and are readily available, unlike my computer. Works for me. This seems to be a constructive routine for me, and I will keep it as long as I continue to be productive. You will want to retain your constructive routines.

A change of pace is not a major disruption; it is doing something different on a trial basis to see if it is right for you, energizing in some way, or has other positive outcomes. It can be almost anything that is different from your usual routine. Here are some suggestions for shaking up your routine. Give one or all of them a try.

Usual Routine	Change To
Attend happy hour	Work out, go home and play with your children or pet, or go for a walk
Turn radio or TV on in the morning	Don't turn them on; think about and plan your day and watch the sunrise
Wait until the last minute to think about meals	Plan your meals and do your grocery shopping in advance
Buy the same brand	Try a different brand (clothes, toiletries, and the like)
Engage in a solitary hobby	Invite someone to share your hobby; take or teach a class or workshop about it
Leave clutter	Pick up after yourself

Drive the same route to and from work	Occasionally drive another route and notice your surroundings
Get your spouse or lover the same type of gift	Ask him for suggestions; think of his likes and dislikes; buy something that is a different type of gift

By now you get the idea and can come up with your own personal change-of-pace ideas. Try them, and if they don't fit or work for you, think of different ones. Just don't give up. Also note how you feel while you try something different and afterward. Some things will not work for you and can be discarded. And, when an idea doesn't work out, you can use that as valuable information.

You now know what to do. A change of pace can be rewarding, but you don't want to have constant change, as that can be stressful. Just enough change every so often and under your control can bring about desirable results.

MINDFULNESS

Becoming mindful teaches you valuable concentration that can help you stay focused on what is truly important in your life. This can be very helpful to you in interactions with your self-absorbed parent, where your heightened emotional state can be distracting or even disabling. Once you get distracted or lost, your parent can gain the advantage and once again you're left with the same old feelings.

Mindfulness is done with conscious thought and intention. You expand your awareness in the moment and notice, appreciate, and even sometimes savor what you are experiencing. This awareness allows you to notice things you didn't notice before, bring something into clearer focus, sort through confusing stimuli and zoom in on important aspects, reduce some anxiety, and you feel more in control. For example, let's suppose that you have practiced mindfulness as described in exercise 6.5 and have become somewhat comfortable and proficient at using it. You decide to try to be more mindful in the next interaction with your self-absorbed parent. You could experience the following:

- You notice that your parent is showing many signs of aging, some of which you don't remember seeing before.

- Your parent is saying the usual hurtful things, but you are not confused about why he is doing this and are able to see the fear your parent has of becoming old and no longer in control.

- The words used by your parent seem meaningless and inaccurate and, although designed to hurt you, are bouncing off you like ball bearings bounce off a wall.

- You are able to discern your parent's anxiety without taking it on or even feeling that you must fix it.

- You are becoming aware that a role shift is in process, and that your parent is fighting it but is also consciously unaware of it.

- You leave the interaction less upset and stressed than usual.

Mindfulness allows you to both expand and contract. You expand your awareness and contract your focus. Practice the following exercise as many times as you possibly can throughout your day. It doesn't take long to do, but you can do it as long as you wish.

Exercise 6.5: Developing Mindfulness

Procedure: This exercise can be done sitting, standing, reclining, walking, and so on. However it is best to be alone in a quiet place.

1. Empty your mind.

2. Don't fight intrusive thoughts.

3. Concentrate on your breathing and how this makes you feel. Try to slow your breath.

4. Become aware of your body, its tense spots, and its pleasurable spots.

5. Focus on what you are experiencing, doing, and feeling. Stay with that and expand your awareness of sensations—seeing, hearing, smelling, touching, and tasting.

6. Notice colors, shapes, forms, sounds, and how your body feels.

7. Continue your expansion as long as you wish.

REDUCE YOUR SELF-ABSORPTION

This suggestion is the basis for entire books on narcissism, but we'll only touch on the subject in this book. The major premise for this suggestion is that self-absorbed behaviors and attitudes are not constructive or helpful. It is important to remember that, just as your self-absorbed parent cannot see his undeveloped narcissism, you are unaware of the behaviors and attitudes you have that are reflective of undeveloped narcissism. Your undeveloped narcissism can do the following:

- Prevent you from detoxifying yourself

- Inhibit you from developing sufficient boundary strength

- Keep you in a position where you can be easily wounded

- Interfere with developing and maintaining meaningful and satisfying relationships

- Get in the way of your reaching out and connecting to others

- Keep you in a defensive state most all of the time

There are many and sufficient reasons to reduce your self-absorption, and when you are able to do so, you will find that you are much less toxic, have better relationships, and are more confident and self-assured. Be aware that this is a lifelong endeavor and that you are mostly unaware of your self-absorbed behaviors and attitudes, but they do have a significant effect on your self and on your relationships.

CHAPTER 7

Strengthen Your Self

Your awareness of your self-absorbed behaviors and attitudes is probably scant or nonexistent. That is, most likely you don't see what you are saying, doing, believing, or thinking that conveys self-absorption. You do understand the negative impact of these, as you have encountered many instances with your self-absorbed parent. You have probably tried to bring these to her attention, but the parent denies these actions and attitudes and is unaware of them. This lack of perception can be difficult to understand, but it's real. She simply cannot see what you and others can see so clearly. That same blindness your parent has about her self-absorption can be true for everyone else, including you. We do not see some parts of ourselves that others can see.

STEPS FOR CHANGE

The first step to reduce or eliminate self-absorbed behaviors and attitudes is to accept a hypothesis that you do have and exhibit some self-absorbed behaviors and attitudes. The second step is to say to yourself that you want to become more aware of these so that you can reduce or eliminate them. Throughout all of this, you must firmly keep in mind that this understanding takes work and is an unfolding process, and that behavior change takes time to develop. Patience with yourself can be helpful as you grow and develop.

After completing (or at least starting) steps one and two, it's time to move on and to identify what you want to change and where you want to grow. The previous chapters provided you with information and strategies to begin, and this chapter focuses on specific self-absorbed behaviors and attitudes and provides some suggestions for changes. It ends with you developing your personal action plan, one that fits you and your circumstances. The specific categories for self-absorption presented in this chapter are as follows:

- Entitlement attitude

- Attention seeking

- Admiration seeking

- Grandiosity

- The impoverished self (grandiosity's flip side)

- Lack of empathy

- Extensions of self

- Demands that others see you as unique and special

- Exploitation of others

- Emptiness at the core of self

Once you become aware of some of your personal self-absorbed behaviors and attitudes, you can take steps to change and thereby reduce or eliminate them.

Entitlement Attitude

An entitlement attitude is demonstrated when you feel that you are supposed to receive preferential treatment and be forgiven for errors, mistakes, or hurting others without penalty or having to feel guilt or shame. The attitude also includes feeling that you can do or say whatever you want to others and they should not object, and that you should receive all or most of the rewards and none of the punishments for what you do. This attitude carries with it the notion that you are to be awarded special considerations and treatment, and that others should agree that you deserve these. It also carries with it an insensitivity to others, an unawareness that others exist and are worthwhile, and an unspoken conviction that others are aware of and accept your specialness and superiority.

REFLECTION: Just in case you unconsciously have and display some version of an entitlement attitude, you can reduce this by becoming more aware of the impact of your behavior on others and by questioning some assumptions you have about how others are supposed to act toward and treat you.

Attention Seeking

Attention-seeking behaviors and attitudes include the following:

- Talking loudly even when you are in a place where your talking will disturb others

- Making grand entrances and exits so that you will be noticed by everyone

- Dressing flamboyantly or in a manner to emphasize body parts

- Doing something to distract from or upstage a person who has the spotlight at that moment

- Starting a fight (verbal)

- Interrupting an ongoing conversation

- Dropping hints and teasers

The intent of these kinds of behaviors is to gain outside validation that you are significant, important, different, and better than others and to reassure yourself that you do indeed exist and are worthwhile. Without attention, self-doubt begins to emerge, you become anxious and maybe even afraid, and this discomfort impels you to act.

REFLECTION: Can you try to validate yourself and reduce your need for external validation? You can become more aware of your attention-seeking behaviors, such as talking loudly, and reduce these.

Admiration Seeking

Admiration seeking refers to the need and yearning for reassurance that you are superior and valued. Behaviors such as boasting, bragging, and fishing for compliments are examples of admiration seeking. Other examples include thinking and feeling that you deserve to be recognized for any of the following:

- As superior to others

- Having talent and ability

- Owning more possessions or more costly ones than others do

- Achieving and accomplishing

- Possessing superior family or other connections (status)

These are a few examples to try to illustrate admiration seeking. It is not so much that these are not laudable things that can and do bring admiration, but that the person seeks to do or focus on them just to gain the admiration of others. Pride in yourself and your accomplishments is appropriate and uplifting. But admiration seeking goes beyond this kind of inner pride to actively seeking and demanding approval, compliments, and even envy from others, and that is a self-absorbed behavior that can be reduced or even eliminated.

REFLECTION: You can compliment yourself and refrain from boasting and bragging. If you truly believe that you are able, accomplished, and did or have something wonderful, that can be enough, and you don't have to have external validation.

Grandiosity

The subtle signs of grandiosity are those that unconsciously reveal the inflated and unrealistic perception of one's self. The person who is grandiose, or has some grandiosity, is unaware of what is being revealed, and even if this is pointed out to her is unlikely to accept that perception. This is indeed an overvaluing of one's self, a feeling of superiority and an expansiveness that does not recognize limitation or boundaries. I'm not talking about the obvious signs of grandiosity that are evident and obvious; rather, I mean the thoughts and ideas that seem reasonable to that person on the surface but in reality are unrealistic, illogical, and irrational. Some examples of this subtle grandiosity are the following:

- Walking into a situation and immediately taking over whatever is being done

- Taking on an excessive number of responsibilities or being unable to say no when you are already overcommitted

- Having the attitude that what you do is better than what others do

- Trying or expecting yourself to be superman or superwoman

- Feeling arrogance

- Feeling contempt for others and that they are inferior

- Failure to see merit in anyone else's ideas or opinions

- Having to have or do it all

You may think that you don't have any undiscovered grandiosity, but it is likely that you are refusing to notice it.

> REFLECTION: Review the list above and be truthful with yourself about your behaviors and attitudes that are reflective of grandiosity. When you find that your thinking and attitudes match those on the list, make a conscious effort to do something different at that moment. The other growth and development strategies, if implemented, can help to reduce your grandiosity.

The Impoverished Self

This is the self that feels deprived, not nurtured, ignored, neglected, or treated unfairly. The important point is how you feel, not what is real. For example, you could be deprived but not feel that way. Or, you could, in fact, be in a position where you aren't nurtured but not have a sense of missing anything. How you perceive your state is what determines if you feel impoverished.

Let's suppose that many of these states are real for you—that is, you are being treated unfairly and you are being ignored. Instead of bemoaning these facts and feeling that you must be unworthy to merit such inattention, it would be more helpful and constructive if you could focus on your strengths, turn your thoughts and energies to something more positive in your life, take steps to make changes that will get you treated fairly and bring you the recognition you deserve, and so on. You don't have to stay mired in your misery.

> REFLECTION: Have you been accused of complaining a lot, even when you think you are just talking about your circumstances and don't see this as complaining? Is it possible that you whine, mope, kvetch, and so on? Are you more focused on what is wrong or miserable about your situation than what is positive and pleasant? You may want to try the following

strategy: Every day for a month, write three pleasant or positive things that you encountered, saw, felt, or experienced that day. At the end of the month, review and take stock of your feelings.

Lack of Empathy

Lack of empathy is a very self-absorbed behavior and attitude that has a serious negative impact on your relationships. Empathy is sensing and feeling at a deep level what the other person is experiencing without becoming enmeshed or overwhelmed by this. You don't just hear the person's words—you feel and understand at a deeper level the meaning behind the words. Listening to content can be important, but the real message is located in the feelings of the speaker, and your ability to be empathic determines if you are able to hear the real message behind the words.

People who have not yet developed their capacity to be empathic can find that they often have difficult relationships, including their intimate relationships. Let's back up a little and note that you cannot be empathic with everyone all of the time. Even gifted and highly experienced therapists cannot do this. Further, it can be dangerous sometimes to be open to receiving feelings from others, especially if you are emotionally susceptible to catching emotions or lack sufficient psychological boundary strength. However, many adults who were not subjected to a parent with a Destructive Narcissistic Pattern (DNP) are able to be empathic with many people some of the time. This topic is discussed in more detail in chapter 9.

REFLECTION: Do you really focus on and listen to others, or do you tend to let your attention and thoughts wander to other things, such as what you intend to say as a response? Do you listen for the feelings behind the other person's words, or are you more focused on what you are feeling?

Extensions of Self

The self-absorbed person is only dimly aware of other people in the world as separate and distinct from her, and at the unconscious level thinks that others exist to serve her. This belief is very much like what infants and children have, but is being acted on by an adult. These self-absorbed people see everything in terms of self, as if they were the only real people in the world and others are only shadows to be ordered around.

This unconscious attitude is also a part of the explanation for why these people do not respect other people's boundaries. They cannot recognize boundaries in others because they consider everything and everyone as a part of them, existing only because they allow them to exist, and under their control. Therefore, they should be allowed to do or say whatever they want to without any objection. Some acts that reflect this attitude include the following:

- Borrowing or taking others' possessions without their permission

- Making social or other arrangements without consultation with other family members

- Making choices and decisions for other people who are able to choose and decide for themselves

- Entering other people's rooms or offices without knocking first and receiving an invitation to enter

- Touching someone without asking permission (children and pregnant women get this a lot)

- Asking personal questions, such as "How much did that cost?" or "When are you getting married?" or "Why don't you have children?"

REFLECTION: Do you consciously or unconsciously violate others' boundaries? Are you always respectful of the other person's privacy, space, and so on? Try to become more aware of when you may violate others' boundaries and when your boundaries are violated.

Perceived as Unique and Special By Others

Everyone wants to be appreciated as a unique, special, and worthwhile person. However, the self-absorbed person takes this desire to an extreme, demanding that everyone respond to her as if she were significantly superior to everyone else in the world. This is the person who thinks that her work, product, talent, or very existence is so far above others' that they can never hope to attain her level. Further, this person is convinced that it is the responsibility of all other people in the world to recognize this specialness and to be admiring and deferential. The self-absorption of this person can blind her to respecting the rights of others or even recognizing that others, too, are worthwhile and unique. Some behaviors and attitudes reflective of this characteristic include the following:

- Making self-aggrandizing comments and remarks

- Constantly pointing out others' faults and flaws

- Frequently speaking of what others should and ought to be and do

- Comparing other people unfavorably to herself

- Blaming others for getting in her way

- Commenting on how she does everything better

- Expecting to be chosen, complimented, and/or recognized for achievements before anyone else

The self-absorbed person who has an underdeveloped appreciation for others and thinks that she is the only unique and special person in the world is unaware of her behaviors and attitudes and of the impact of these on others.

REFLECTION: You know that you are unique and special, but are you fully aware that others are also unique and special? Do you constantly promote yourself and fail to recognize others' accomplishments? How can you become more aware of what you are doing, saying, and believing?

Exploitation of Others

Using others to gain personal benefits is exploitation. Coupled with this is the attitude and conviction that others are not worthy, they exist to serve the exploiter, and they are inferior to her. While people with a DNP exploit everyone in some way, the people closest to them are the ones who suffer the most because the relationship is used to promote and support the exploitation. The self-absorbed person is capitalizing on others' caring, concern, good nature, desire to please, need for approval, and other such relationship factors. This is done to meet the personal needs of the person with a DNP and to the detriment of the other person. What are some exploitive acts?

- Borrowing money without paying it back

- Expecting favors without reciprocation

- Urging, cajoling, or persuading someone to do something that is not in that person's best interests but is something where the self-absorbed person gains

- Lying, cheating, distorting, and misleading to gain an advantage

- Using "If you loved me" or "If you cared about me" to get someone to do something that person doesn't want to do

There are many other exploitive acts, and you can probably add to the list, especially if you have a self-absorbed parent. Does, or did, your parent do any of the following?

- Expect you to drop what you are doing to do something for her

- Expect you to make her wants and needs your highest priority

- Blame you for her discomfort or misery

- Use guilt or shame to manipulate you to do things you do not want to do

- Criticize you for not reading her mind and giving or doing what she wants or needs

- Expect you to live up to her vision of herself

Now, let's turn those behaviors and attitudes around to get an idea of how you may be exploiting others. I know you don't believe that you are, but you may not be aware of these behaviors and attitudes in yourself. Look at all the items in both lists, and reflect on what you do and say in your closest family, work, social, and/or intimate relationships that is similar to items in these lists. These are the behaviors and attitudes you can work to change.

REFLECTION: How much do you like to be able to trump others, and what are you willing to do to ensure that you come out on top or as a winner? Do you unintentionally exploit relationships for your gain? Do you try to get people to do things for you just because you want them to? Are you sensitive to the potential you may have for exploiting your relationships?

Shallow Emotions

Adults with healthy narcissism can experience and express a wide and deep variety of emotions. In contrast, self-absorbed adults are extremely limited in experiencing and expressing their feelings. Experiencing for them seems to be mainly limited to fear and anger, and while they have the words when expressing other feelings, they don't have the accompanying emotions. These people are not genuine in their expression of feelings, except for the variations of fear and anger.

To get an idea of your range and level for experiencing and expressing emotions, complete the following exercise.

Exercise 7.1: Experiencing and Expressing

Materials: A sheet of paper and a pen or pencil for writing

Procedure: Find a place to complete this exercise where you will not be distracted or disturbed.

1. Start with your awakening time and make a list of the hours of your yesterday from beginning to end on the left side of the paper. You can use whole hours or half hours. Leave some vertical space between them.

   6:00 AM

   7:00 AM

   8:00 AM

2. Beside each time period, make a column list of all the feelings you remember experiencing.

   6:00 AM   sleepy

                   pleased

                   pensive

3. Beside the feelings column, list the names of people to whom you expressed any of these feelings verbally and directly.

4. Review the emotions you experienced and the emotions you expressed. You may be surprised to find one of the following:

   ■ You expressed few feelings openly and directly.

- You did not communicate many of your feelings to someone.

- You had little variability in what you felt.

- You primarily expressed negative feelings.

- You were primarily aware of experiencing negative feelings.

- You have a very short feelings vocabulary list.

REFLECTION: You may be too focused on negative feelings and want to increase the number of positive feelings you experience and express. Try to develop a larger vocabulary of feeling words.

Emptiness at the Core of Self

This state is difficult to describe because "empty" is usually defined as the absence of something and often denotes some sort of boundary (the edges of an empty hole, for example). The psychological state of emptiness is also an absence, but without borders or defining points, and that makes it even more difficult to describe. There is nothing. The following description does not fully capture the emptiness of self-absorbed people, as this is being defined as a lack of all or most of the following. Self-absorbed people do not have:

- Connection to others that is meaningful

- Connection to the universe (inspiration/spirituality)

- The capacity for varied and deep feelings

- An understanding of what others are experiencing

- Compassion, mercy, and the like

- An appreciation for beauty and wonder

- An understanding and feeling of self as separate and distinct and as having value and worth

- A capacity for loving and cherishing oneself and others

- The ability to transcend oneself for others

The empty person does not know any other state and assumes that others feel empty inside, as she does. No one outside the person can provide what is lacking—that has to come from within each person. But the person may not really even realize what's missing, only that she needs something to fill the void.

Many people who do not have a DNP may have some voids at the core of self. However, they recognize what is lacking and take steps to try to get what is needed. People with a DNP are completely, or almost completely, empty at the core and can sense a lack but cannot identify what is lacking. They think that others have something they do not, and they try to get it but fail because they don't know what they are trying to get. Instead of reflection and growing the self, some people substitute activity. Other substitutions include the following:

- Substance abuse

- Blind allegiance to a "calling" such as a cult, religion, or charismatic person

- Gambling

- Overeating or undereating

- Shopping and overspending

- Overcommitment to civic, social, and other such activities that fill the time

The void is never filled by these activities, and these people continue to try to find something to combat the emptiness.

Since almost everyone can have some lacks or holes, what prevents and overcomes emptiness? Think about constructive and enriching activities, behaviors, and attitudes that could help fill your holes. Some examples are:

- Meaningful, satisfying, and enduring relationships

- Meaning and purpose for one's life

- A rich and satisfying inspirational aspect of life

- Reaching out and touching others to enrich their lives

- Expanding the self to be creative, empathic, and wise

REFLECTION: Are you aware of your holes? Are you using constructive means to fill these, or are you relying on unconstructive actions? What can you do to enrich your life?

GOALS TO BECOME LESS SELF-ABSORBED

It can be helpful to visualize and articulate some goals for changing your self-absorbed behaviors and attitudes to those that are self-reflective instead. *Self-reflective* means here that you think, act, and feel in accord with what is sufficient for you, but you are also able to act to put other people's well-being ahead of yours when you judge it to be necessary. You don't sacrifice your self for others, but you do give of yourself when their need is greater than yours, and you consciously decide to do so. You take care of your self, adequately protect it, and are able to reach out to others. You cease an unconscious belief that you are the center of everything and that all else revolves around you. You reduce your actions that speak of self-absorption, and you increase your actions that speak of your awareness of others as worthwhile, unique, and separate and distinct from you.

Following are some possible goals and suggestions for changes in behavior. Change your behavior and you tend to change your attitude. Try to visualize what you will do and say that lets you know you've reached your goal for reducing or eliminating a possible self-absorbed behavior and attitude. Remember that if you do have a particular self-absorbed behavior and attitude, you are probably not consciously aware of it. That's why it's important that you carefully consider all of the suggestions.

Characteristics of the Self-Absorbed	Suggestions
Entitlement attitude	Wait your turn. Don't give orders or demands. Don't expect others to do for you what you can do for yourself. Don't seek unearned credit.
Attention seeking	Let the attention come to you. Make quiet entrances and exits. Don't interrupt others. Speak quietly.
Admiration seeking	Cultivate internal pleasure for your accomplishments. Cease boasting and bragging. Let compliments come to you without fishing for them. Don't always have a personal story to tell.
Grandiosity	Recognize and accept your personal limitations. Learn to say no and stick to it. Reflect on a need to be superior and reduce or eliminate it.
Impoverished self	Resolve to stop complaining, whining, and the like, and to act on things that can be changed or resolved. Let go of fretting over

	things that cannot be changed or resolved.
Lack of empathy	Stop talking and listen. Focus on the speaker. Try to hear the feelings and meaning behind the words.
Extensions of self	Work to have strong and resilient boundaries. Respect others' rights and space. Don't ask favors. Don't expect others to follow your orders. Make requests instead of orders or demands.
Demands that others perceive you as unique and special	Appreciate others' contributions. Recognize that others, too, are special.
Exploitation of others	Become more independent, return favors, and treat others fairly. Don't lie, cheat, distort, or mislead.
Shallow emotions	Develop a list of feeling words and try to use a new one each day. Stop periodically to reflect on what you are experiencing at that moment.
Emptiness at the core	Complete exercises 7.2 and 7.3 in this book, perform altruistic acts, reflect on any "holes" that may exist.

BEYOND SELF-ABSORPTION: MEANING AND PURPOSE

Once you are on your way to reducing your self-absorption and building healthy adult narcissism, including self-reflection, you will also want to develop more meaning and purpose in your life. Meaning and purpose expand the richness of our lives, connect us to the wider universe, and help us enjoy life. There are many positive benefits:

- Reducing or eliminating isolation and alienation

- Combating despair, hopelessness, and helplessness

- Accepting ourselves as we are and working to effect positive changes

- Developing more realistic expectations of oneself and others

- Learning the limits of your personal responsibility

- Becoming more centered and grounded

Let's do a checkup on the meaning and purpose in your life.

Exercise 7.2: Checking In on Your Meaning and Purpose

Materials: A set of crayons, felt markers, or colored pencils; several sheets of large newsprint or other paper for drawing; paper and a pen or pencil for writing

Procedure: You will create a drawing for each part of your life.

1. Do each one separately and take a few moments to close your eyes and really focus on or experience each before drawing a picture, symbol, or abstract expression for the topic or item.

   - Two or more of your close relationships. Draw as many of these as you wish.

   - Your career, job, or work

   - Your inspirational or spiritual life

   - Your emotional self and life

- The enjoyment in your life

- Your creative works, hobbies, or recreation

2. You will have seven or more drawings. Spread the drawings out on a table or floor, or tape them to a wall. Look carefully at your drawings as a group and see how satisfied or how dissatisfied you are with your life as depicted by these experiences.

3. Put the drawings in two piles, one called "Satisfactory" and the other, "Needs Work." Take the Needs Work pile, note the content, and write a description of your feelings about each item in this pile. For example, you may have your enjoyment, hobbies, and career in this pile, and you would write about your feelings about each of these. Take the Satisfactory pile and repeat the procedure.

4. Take a new sheet of paper and draw a line down the middle, labeling one side "Increase These" and the other side "Decrease These." List the actions you can take—either increasing positive ones or decreasing negative ones—that will lead to more satisfaction in the parts of your life that need work. For example, for the Increase These section of the Enjoyment aspect of your life, you may list things like attending plays, concerts, and other events you like. In your Decrease These section for the same aspect, you could write, "Letting chores eat up my spare time by finding another way to get them done or by changing my need to get them done at a particular time." In other words, you are developing an action plan to improve those aspects of your life that are not as satisfactory as you would like.

5. The final step is to draw a picture of your ideal life given where you are right now and the resources available to you. Try not to fantasize about the improbable, such as winning the lottery, or the impossible, such as being able to change another person.

If you completed the exercise, you now have a clearer awareness of some aspects of your life that can have meaning and purpose for you, where you are satisfied or pleased, and where you are dissatisfied or displeased. You have developed some actions you can take to become more satisfied. You may also have a clearer vision of what and how you want your life to be and can visualize how you can achieve it. Now let's take a look at the benefits of embarking on this work.

Reducing Isolation and Alienation

Isolation and alienation involve a psychological and emotional distancing of yourself from others; feeling disconnected and alone; lacking direction, meaning, and purpose for your life; and not being able to see how you can effect positive changes. Although this description may sound like depression, it does not have the clinical and physical aspects of depression. This is an existential dilemma that everyone can experience off and on throughout life. It has no definitive answer—only momentary ones—and can emerge when your life's meaning and purpose are not to your satisfaction.

Feeling isolated or alienated is akin to being adrift in the universe with no reference points for locating yourself. Some of common reference points are the following:

- Meaningful and satisfying relationships

- Enjoyment, pleasure, and delight

- A sense of being wanted and needed

- The knowledge that your contributions are appreciated and helpful

- The feeling of being competent and effective in many aspects of your life

When one or more of these reference points are missing, you can begin to feel alone and cut off from other people. These feelings can intensify until they become feelings of being isolated and alienated.

Materials: Several sheets of paper and a pen or pencil for writing

Procedure:

1. Write down all of the reference points in the previous list, leaving some vertical space between them.

2. Under each item, list two or more such items that relate to you. For example, under enjoyment you could list home, work, social events, and the like, or something like books, play, and sports. It's your choice.

3. Now rate your satisfaction with each item and subitem using a scale from 0 (extremely dissatisfied) to 10 (extremely satisfied).

4. Make a list of all items and subitems rated below 5. These are items that need work.

5. Look at your lists and ratings and judge how isolated and alienated you are feeling right now. Use 0-extremely; 1-very; 2-most of time; 3-some of time; 4-infrequently and 5-not at all.

Combating Despair, Helplessness, and Hopelessness

Milder versions of despair include discouragement and dejection. A milder form of helplessness might be called a sense of being ineffectual or impotent. As for hopelessness, milder versions include feeling incurable and that things are impossible and bleak. I'm introducing these milder forms because you may not have the intense version of these feelings but could be suffering some of their less extreme manifestations. These, too, can contribute to a sense of reduced meaning and purpose for your life.

Despair, helplessness, and hopelessness refer to your perception of your effectiveness in your life and your ability to control what you think you should. This last perception is the one that may be fueling your discouragement, dejection, or despair. You may want to refer back to the discussion about extensions of self at this point— that is, when you think that other people are, or should be, under your control. When they don't do what you want them to, this can produce feelings of being ineffectual. You fail to accept that they were not, are not, and will not be under your control. You have an unrealistic expectation, some underdeveloped narcissism that needs work so that you more fully understand and accept at an unconscious level that others are separate and distinct from you. Then you can give up the fantasy that others should do what you want them to do.

There are many uncontrollable things in life, such as the economy, your talents and ability, what other people say and do, and so on. Some things are just too large and complex to be under anyone's control, like wars. You must develop a realistic perception of what is and what is not under your control. This change will not prevent you from feeling discouraged, but it will prevent you from feeling despairing, helpless, and hopeless. However, you will have to give up fantasies that you have power and control over any of the following. You cannot:

- Make someone love you

- Cause others to change

- Expect the world to always be fair and just

- Realistically expect preferential treatment

- Control what others say and do

- Think of yourself as the only one in the universe

Acceptance of Self and Positive Changes

You may have become more aware of some previously hidden aspects of yourself as you've read this book and completed the exercises. There may also be some behaviors and attitudes you became aware of that could be changed, and you may have some aspect of yourself about which you feel embarrassed or shamed. Not to worry—everyone has this experience and can always use more growing and developing, especially to develop healthy adult narcissism.

Your challenge will be to accept yourself as you are: needed changes, shame, and all. Try not to deny, minimize, rationalize, or exaggerate any aspects of yourself. Above all, don't get discouraged at the amount of work you need to do, as that will retard progress. It's much more helpful to focus your thoughts and energies on positives for the most part rather than dwelling on negatives.

Some self-talk can help you with your self-acceptance. By using positive self-talk, you're not ignoring or excusing what you perceive to be faults and flaws. Instead, you are working with them to effect positive changes. It is very important to have patience with yourself and to persevere in the face of failure or setbacks. Try some or all of the following self-talk.

Thoughts or Behavior	Self-Talk
You are less than perfect in doing something.	It was good enough.
You make a mistake.	I'll do better next time.
You fail or encounter barriers.	I'll try harder.
You think you can't or won't succeed.	I'll do the very best I am able to do.
You feel responsible for others' feelings.	I don't need to always take care of others.

| You become aware of your self-absorbed behaviors and attitudes. | I am working on this, and I'll overcome many of these. |
| You become concerned or discouraged about your progress. | Look at what I have been able to do so far! I will continue to work on me. |

Developing More Realistic Expectations

You may need to develop more realistic expectations for yourself and for others. For example, you may expect perfection of yourself, and by extension may also expect that of others. These expectations are unrealistic and can lead you to:

- Blame yourself or others when mistakes are made or something is not perfect

- Do and say things that negatively affect a relationship when your expectations are not met, especially when these expectations are not specified, and you expect the other person to read your mind

- Become shamed and displace this on others around you

- Remain in a constant state of anxiety that you will make a mistake

All of these can affect your health, your self-perception, and your relationships.

Expectations are generally shoulds and oughts. For instance, you may feel and say that others "should" do things your way when it would be perfectly reasonable to let them do things their way, for example, loading the dishwasher. Further, you can have an unrealistic expectation that others "ought" to know what you want or need and meet that want or need without you having to say a word. It can be pleasing for you when this happens but can be destructive when you expect it.

On the other hand, it must be noted that having high expectations for yourself can be positive. Note that I said high expectations—not unrealistic ones. For example, there is nothing wrong with seeking perfection and trying hard to attain it. What is negative, however, is when you demand it of yourself and of others (these do seem to go together in many cases), and when you cannot accept less than perfection. Since perfection is rarely if ever attained, you remain dissatisfied with yourself and with others. Your relationships suffer, since others don't have your drive for perfection and can be satisfied with being good enough while working to improve. This latter mind-set does not produce blame, shame, constant anxiety, and dissatisfaction, and this is sufficient reason to try to adopt more realistic expectations for yourself and for others.

Limits of Your Personal Responsibility

If you have not internalized that there are limits to your personal responsibility, then you have not fully come to know yourself as separate and distinct from others. Further, you may be unnecessarily accepting blame, experiencing shame, perceiving yourself as ineffectual, and trying to maintain control over people and events that you cannot truly control. These issues relate to your boundary strength. Whereas resilient boundaries are desirable, you may have soft, rigid, or spongy boundaries. *Whose Life Is It Anyway? When to Stop Taking Care of Their Feelings and Start Taking Care of Your Own* (Brown 2002) discusses this in more detail and presents strategies that can begin to help you build sufficient boundary strength.

Some examples may help to clarify how you perceive your personal responsibility:

■ Do you apologize or say you did not intend to do that when someone says that you caused her to feel a particular feeling?

- Can you be assertive when someone insists that you do something you do not want to do?

- Have you violated your personal standards, ethics, or values to please another person or because you did not want to disappoint someone?

- Do you feel bad (shamed or guilty) when another person feels uncomfortable?

- Do you put yourself out to ensure others' comfort or pleasure?

- Do you suppress your feelings and/or needs so that others will not be burdened?

If many or all of these fit you, then you are taking unwarranted responsibility. You don't know, accept, or recognize that there are limits to your duty and need to care for others. It's not that you don't have some responsibility to be tactful, sensitive, and understanding of others; you do, and that can strengthen relationships. However, the acts, feelings, and attitudes described above are indicators that you have gone too far in your efforts to connect, and that when you do these things you are not taking care of yourself. For example, you do not cause someone to have a particular feeling. People choose to feel a particular way for a variety of reasons that are not under your control. Yes, something in their environment may trigger their feeling, but it remains their feeling, not your responsibility.

Becoming Centered and Grounded

This chapter has focused on reducing self-absorption and describing what benefits you can gain from your continuing self-development. All of these, and some others benefits that are described in the next chapter, can lead to your becoming more centered and grounded. Doing so can help you in many ways:

- You don't lose your way and go off in a direction that is not constructive and beneficial to a meaningful and purposeful life.

- You choose to act in accord with your values and can resist manipulation by others.

- You do not fly apart, melt down, or become isolated during troubling times or in crises.

- You are able to maintain your sense of your self under very trying and distressful circumstances.

- You are able to tolerate being alone without feeling lonely.

- You choose relationships that are mutually beneficial.

- You build on your strengths and work on what you want to change about yourself.

- You are able to resist becoming mired in despair, hopelessness, and helplessness.

When you are centered and grounded, you are able to encounter and experience life's vicissitudes with some confidence that you will survive. You'll do the best you can and are assured that what you do and what you are is good enough, even when you don't succeed to the extent you wanted to. You are comfortable with yourself, you like yourself, you are able to accept your imperfections without feeling that they are shameful and must be hidden at all costs, and you are able to let others manage and control their own lives, thoughts, and feelings. Becoming centered and grounded has a lot of positive effects on you and on your life.

Becoming centered and grounded will also prevent you from becoming narcissistically wounded frequently or most of the time. Nothing will entirely eliminate your being wounded, but you can reduce your vulnerability by building your self and by developing healthy adult narcissism and strong and resilient boundaries. But you will always have a little more personal growing and developing to do, and that means you may be wounded on occasion. Further, you will find that being centered and grounded makes it easier to do the following:

- Let go of resentment, grudges, and the like

- Ward off incorporating, identifying with, and acting on others' projections (projective identification)

- Accept and tolerate differences of others

- Initiate and maintain meaningful and satisfying relationships

- Have a meaningful and purposeful life

The next chapter provides suggestions and strategies that are designed to promote your personal growth and development so that you can let go of even more painful events and can move further in getting over what has been festering for some time. You've probably let go of some hurt, resentment, and grudges from some past experiences, but you may be not be rid of all of them. You may also have reduced or eliminated your feelings about these and some of the lingering negative effects. This is considerable progress, and you can compliment yourself for your efforts and achievements. There is more to do, but you are really on your way.

CHAPTER 8

Your Ideal Self: Determine the Person You Want to Be

Instantaneous change is possible but not very probable, as you are a complex person with many facets of your self, some of which are unknown to you. So, trying to make major changes all at once is probably not a good idea, since success at all of them is unlikely and that can be discouraging. What I propose is that you try to make small changes over time. As you become more aware of your thoughts, attitudes, behaviors, self-absorption, strengths, weaknesses, and boundary strength, and the extent of your narcissistic wounding, your changes can expand at an even greater rate.

STRATEGIES FOR GROWTH

This chapter will present strategies for changes that can fortify your self, making it less vulnerable to becoming wounded by your self-absorbed parent. We'll also focus on building some underdeveloped parts of your self. You've received some suggestions throughout the book, and here are even more. Some may not fit or be feasible for you, and it is not reasonable for you to use these. Go with the suggestions that make sense to you at this time. Later, after you've made some initial progress, you can return to those you put aside and see if they can be of use.

We'll be examining six categories for suggested shifts: building awareness, reducing self-absorption, increasing self-reflection, cultivating your strengths, developing strong and resilient boundaries, and becoming your own person.

Build Awareness

An aware person experiences himself as a fully functioning human who is mindful of the transitory nature of life and also has a sense of the following:

- Appreciating the present
- Being part of the universe
- Seeing wonder and beauty in the world
- Sensing the messages of the body
- Listening with attention
- Responding with the mind and body in unison
- Choosing standards and principles
- Accepting reality
- Accessing and identifying feelings

Appreciating the present. This capacity helps you to more fully be in the "now" of your existence. The past is important and influences the present, but the past is not necessarily relevant to the here and now. The future is an unknown, and how much it will be experienced is a guess at best, so speculation about that is futile and can detract from the full experience of the here and now.

Being part of the universe. This is a part of feeling connected, less isolated and alone, and a part of something larger than yourself. It is also important in having the capacity to love and to be loved. You feel that you have some impact and influence, and that you are not totally at the mercy of forces that you cannot see, understand, or control. The vastness of the universe is daunting but not threatening. There is much to discover.

Seeing wonder and beauty in the world. Someone with this ability is able to focus on the promise, not the negativity. It's easy to get caught up in the unfairness of people and situations, feel helpless and powerless to effectively deal with adversity, and begin to feel hopeless and despairing. These negatives are easy to find. What is harder to focus on are the positives, such as wonder and beauty. Try to look around you and notice wonder and beauty several times every day.

Sensing the messages of the body. When you cultivate this ability, you'll find it easier to stay centered and grounded and to better understand your inner world. You can know what reactions you are having and have some understanding of why you react as you do. You'll have a firmer grasp on the influences of your past and your personality and can be accepting of these, even as you are trying to change some things about yourself.

Listening with attention. Attending allows you to be fully emotionally present when listening to others and to avoid distraction by inner or external concerns. This ability allows you to hear the overt and hidden messages in the communication, to connect with the person in a meaningful way, and to better understand what that person is experiencing. You are not asking questions instead of responding empathically. You are not distracted with your thoughts of other matters. You do not change the topic or do anything but use your thoughts and feelings to listen to the other person.

Responding with the mind and body in unison. The mind is not doing one thing while the body does something else. Rather, the two stay in touch with each other. This symmetry contributes to mindfulness and awareness.

Choosing standards and principles. Choose what you believe and value instead of unconsciously acting on old programming, what you were taught, what others find to be of importance and have imposed, or opinions that can distort current reality. This is not to say that standards and principles from the past are discarded. In fact, these can be kept but are now openly and directly chosen by you, not blindly accepted. New ones are added that fit your current situation and the person you are now.

Accepting reality. When you accept reality, you don't romanticize it or deny the negative or positive aspects, and you can recognize how your perception could be distorted. The depressing aspects of reality are not ignored, nor are they emphasized to the extent that it seems futile to continue. Acceptance of reality is an adult response and can be a source of motivation to act to make the reality as constructive as possible.

Accessing and identifying feelings. This is a major accomplishment, and one that contributes to a better understanding of yourself and of others. These emotions are neither shallow nor few in number. You are not fearful of knowing what you are feeling at all times, and this is a valuable source of information about what you are understanding and sensing. Your feelings are not always rational and logical, but that doesn't mean that they are not informative and valuable.

ACKNOWLEDGE YOUR PROGRESS

Building awareness has already begun by your completing some or all of the exercises in the book. You are probably much more attuned to what you are experiencing at a given moment, how your family of origin and past experiences influenced who you are and how you think and feel, the extent of your psychological boundary strength and resilience, and maybe even some of your underdeveloped narcissism. You have explored what gives meaning and purpose to your life and other positive attributes that can help keep you centered and grounded. These are major accomplishments. However, there is more that can be done to help you become the kind of person you envision. Strategies for building your awareness include the following:

- Periodically and silently ask yourself to identify and label what you are experiencing.

- Try to sense what other people may be feeling.

- Stay alert to your reactions as being the result of projection or transference.

- Realize that your feelings may be misleading.

- Remind yourself of the limits of your personal responsibility when interacting with others.

You are entitled to your feelings, and no one else has a right to feel or suggest that you are wrong for having them. They are yours and should be respected. However, you can be misled by your feelings when you factor in your personality, family-of-origin and other past experiences, the extent of your self-absorption, and your emotional susceptibility. These are some major influences that determine what feelings are triggered for you. You may not be reacting to the present objective reality, but instead be unconsciously reacting to these major factors. Staying aware of their possible influences can moderate your internal responses (some negative feelings may become less intense), help you make more constructive external responses, reduce any tendency you may have to personalize what others say and do, and help you learn to attend to others instead of usually having your concern and attention on yourself.

DISCERN BETWEEN THOUGHTS AND FEELINGS

Learn to identify the difference between your thoughts and your feelings. All too often, people tend to confuse the two and are unable to identify what they are feeling. Also, they may unconsciously defend against whatever they are feeling at the moment by suppression, repression, denial, transference, or projection, to name a few defenses. It's okay to defend against a feeling, but it then becomes more helpful to explore why the feeling may be a threat to you. This exploration process that can contribute to building your awareness.

Let's go back to the notion that you can confuse thoughts with feelings. Add to that the tendency some people have to jump to conclusions about their experiences without ever being aware of what they are feeling, and you can begin to better understand how you may have cut yourself off from awareness that could be helpful.

Thoughts and Conclusions	Possible Feelings
I don't like this (him).	I am fearful that I'm in danger.
I'm uncomfortable.	I am unsettled, disquieted, or anxious.
I am comfortable.	I feel in control, safe, protected, or cared for.
You are lovable.	I have strong affectionate caring and concern for you.
I feel bad when you cry.	I get in touch with my inadequacy, powerlessness, helplessness, and I feel guilty or ashamed.
I feel upbeat.	I am pleased, happy, and so on.

When you read the thoughts and conclusions in this list, you may think that what the person is feeling is obvious and that everyone will know what is meant. However, each thought or conclusion would need clarification for others to really understand what that particular person means by that statement. For example, the statement "I'm uncomfortable" could mean any of the following, or even something else:

- This chair doesn't fit, and I have to squirm around so that I don't hurt.

- I have a cold and my sinuses are congested.

- Something about this situation is arousing my sense of potential danger.

- I am working hard to keep my irritation hidden.

- I am overheated.

- I am cold

- I am hungry.

This list could go on for a while, as there are many internal and external conditions that explain the thought or conclusion "I'm uncomfortable." Some, such as a sense of danger, would need to be internally explored further so that you better understood what in the environment was producing this feeling of being in danger for you. This exploration of your feeling to clarify it helps you to know what action you can take to reduce your discomfort.

When you increase your awareness of what you are experiencing and feeling, you can find that you are better able to pick up on what others are experiencing. You become more sensitive and aware of others when you shift your focus from yourself outward, to another person. So, there are personal and relationship reasons to work on building your awareness. You can better understand yourself and you can better understand others.

Reduce Self-Absorption

Developing healthy adult narcissism is where you decrease your self-absorbed behaviors and attitudes and, at the same time, increase your self-reflection. Both are critical to prevent and reduce narcissistic wounding. It may seem like a paradox to both focus on your self and get out of your self, but a cohesive centered and grounded self involves both. Try the following exercise to develop your personal set of suggestions for reducing self-absorption.

Exercise 8.1: Reduce Self-Absorption

Materials: Six sheets of paper and a pen or pencil for writing

Procedure: Complete all six steps first, because you may be blind to some of your self-absorbed behaviors and attitudes. Step 7 provides the alternate thinking that can help reduce self-absorbed behaviors and attitudes.

1. Write the phrase "Admiration Seeking" at the top of one page. Below that, list some qualities about yourself that you think are admirable. Don't be modest when forming your list. When your list is complete, close your eyes and visualize receiving compliments about these qualities from yourself.

2. Write "Unique and Special" at the top of another page. List events, times, and places, in which you feel or felt unique and special. Next, list qualities about yourself that you think are unique and special. When you have completed these, close your eyes and visualize being recognized for your qualities.

3. Write "Grandiosity" at the top of another page.

   a. List your strengths, such as "I can organize and plan," "I like to get things completed," "I'm outgoing and sociable," "I'm quiet and reserved," and so on.

   b. Beside each strength on your list, write how the strength can or does cause potential limitations for you. For example, if one of your strengths is organizing and planning, a limitation can be that you have to depend on others to carry out the plans. The strength of being outgoing and sociable could have a limitation of not recognizing others' space or boundaries. It may take a little thought, but you can discern possible limitation for each strength.

   c. Beside, or at the end of, each limitation, list a feeling you've experienced or think you would have when you encounter that limitation. For example, if you encounter having to depend on others to implement plans, the feeling could be frustration.

4. Write "Entitlement" at the top of another page. List some specific situations in the past when you felt you did not receive what you wanted, needed, or deserved. You may want to limit the time frame for your list, list only major items, or list only the experiences that produced the most intense feelings for you. Review your list and put a check by the items where you felt, thought, or expected to receive preferential attention, extra consideration, more than others received, and so on.

5. Write "Attention Seeking" at the top of the next page. Visualize yourself in each of the following situations and list the feelings you experience as you do the visualization. Complete each visualization before moving on to the next one.

   a. Your work group is holding a meeting, and you are a little late arriving. As you enter the room, a few people look at you, but most are focused on the speaker, who is one of your peers.

   b. Your neighbor, a colleague at work, tells you about his son's award for academic excellence.

   c. You are attending a party where most of the attention seems to be on the couple who are houseguests of the host and hostess. You can't seem to get a sustained conversation going with anyone.

6. Write "Exploitation of Others" at the top of the next page. Recall the previous week and list all the favors you requested; what you asked, ordered, or demanded that others do for you that you could have done for yourself; when or if you took advantage of someone's good nature; and/or if you got someone to do something he did not want to do.

7. Review what you wrote for steps 1 through 6.

   a. On the page titled "Admiration Seeking," now write, "I can admire some things about myself and I don't have to have others admire me."

b. On the page titled "Unique and Special," write, "I am unique and special, but so are other people."

c. On the page titled "Grandiosity," write, "I have many strengths, but these also have limitations. I have limits on what I can control."

d. On the page titled "Entitlement," write, "I am entitled to ask for what I want or need and to work for that, but others have no obligation to give it to me. I will respect others' rights."

e. On the page titled "Attention Seeking," write, "I don't have to have attention all, or most, of the time."

f. On the page titled "Exploitation of Others," write, "I can become more independent, do things for myself, ask people to do only what they want to do, and accept their refusals, and I can recognize and respect others' differences."

One additional step you can take, if you choose, is to write the items in number 7, on a 3 by 5-inch index card. Put it in an accessible place and review it weekly.

Here are some specific acts that can help reduce self-absorption and increase self-reflection:

- Start every conversation about a topic other than you. Save your personal stories and concerns for your nearest and dearest.

- Don't interrupt conversations.

- Knock before entering a room, even if the door is open, and wait for an invitation to enter.

- Touch only with permission. This includes children. Hold your arms out and let them choose. Ask for a hug, and accept a no.

- Ask yourself frequently, "Is this about me?"

- Don't take everything personally, even when it is meant that way.

- Examine when you smile. Is it most often when you or others are talking about you, or when you are thinking about something connected to you? Try smiling at and for others.

Increase Self-Reflection

Self-reflection is a way to examine what you are doing, feeling, and thinking to determine if you are unconsciously exhibiting self-absorbed behaviors and attitudes, if your boundaries are appropriately strong and resilient, if you are neglecting to take into account the needs of the other person, or if you are in danger of becoming enmeshed or overwhelmed. Yes, self-reflection is focused on yourself, but in a different way than when you are self-absorbed. Examine the following to get an idea of the distinction.

Self-Absorbed	Self-Reflective
Am I doing it right?	I'm doing it okay, but can I improve.
I'm afraid of saying something wrong.	I want to respond appropriately and will try to tune in to what the other person is feeling.
I must be perfect.	I'll do my best, and I'll accept that I may not be perfect.
I made a mistake, and that's awful.	I can and will do better.
Others must like and approve of me or I am doomed to be rejected.	I want to be liked and receive approval, but not at the expense of my integrity or values.

Cultivate Your Strengths

Many people have unrecognized and/or unused strengths, and you may be no exception. You may emphasize your faults and flaws more than you celebrate your strengths. After all, these perceived shortcomings are your shame, and you work to overcome having to feel this most uncomfortable feeling. What I want to suggest is that you begin to make a shift toward emphasizing and cultivating your strengths. That shift doesn't mean that you ignore your shortcomings, flaws, and the like. No, you will continue to work on these, but you will also take a fresh look at your strengths so that you can better capitalize on them. It is much easier to build on strengths than it is to remediate weaknesses or deficits. This process will also lead you to greater and more realistic self-acceptance and help to fortify you against external assaults, such as demeaning and devaluing remarks.

What are your strengths? You listed some if you completed the previous exercise, but you probably have some you are overlooking, and you may not even be aware of others. If you are like many people, you think of your strengths in terms of what others have noticed or things about which you've been complimented. That can be limiting because you cannot always count on others to comment on or compliment your strengths. Further, you may have some flaws or weaknesses that you don't realize are concealing strengths. For example, some people may think that focusing on details is a weakness, and it can be when carried to excess. But embedded in that behavior and attitude is the strength of being able to reduce or eliminate mistakes. Indeed, in some professions and jobs it is essential that the primary focus be on details (for example, preparing the room for surgery, food presentation, events planning, proofreading, strategic bombing, and so on).

Some more examples may be helpful.

Flaw or Weakness	Possible Embedded Strength
Makes blunt direct comments	Genuine; leaves little doubt as to what is meant
Stubborn	Has the courage of his convictions; maintains personal values; decisive
Dreamy	Imaginative; visualizes possibilities
Indecisive	Alert to many possible options and alternatives; takes time to consider pros and cons for each option

Now it's your turn to try to determine some of your unrecognized strengths.

Exercise 8.2: Finding Your Strengths

Materials: A sheet of paper and a pen or pencil for writing

Procedure: Find a place to work where you will not be disturbed.

1. Make a list of your perceived weaknesses and faults. If you have been criticized for some behaviors and attitudes, also list these, even if you don't agree with them.

2. Beside each item you listed for step 1, write a possible strength that could be embedded. Some may not include a strength, but most will. Do the best that you can.

You now have list of strengths to cultivate. As you focus on and cultivate these strengths, you can reduce, moderate, or eliminate the flaw or weakness. Let's go back to the example of attention to details to get some notion of how this can work. The strength could be a reduction of possible errors or mistakes. Therefore, you could work to reduce these but also set a personal limit for how much checking and attention is good enough, acceptable, and the like. You could also start to realize and accept that others do not have this characteristic and that it is not reasonable to demand that others also have this attention to detail. In other words, accept it about yourself, but don't expect others to have it. Then, too, you would want to take care that the need to attend to details doesn't become excessive. Let's see how the strengths in the examples could be cultivated.

Strength	Cultivation
Genuine	Operate with tact and concern for others' emotional states.
Decisive	Make informed decisions; don't jump to conclusions.
Imaginative	Start to create some of the possibilities you imagine.
Alert to many possibilities	Set a personal time limit for considering pros and cons, then make a decision and forget the other alternatives.

Develop Strong and Resilient Boundaries

Your psychological boundaries define where you are differentiated from others, and they protect you from external assaults, such as others' projections that can lead to projective identifications. Thus, having strong and resilient boundaries is critical to all of the following relationship-enhancing thoughts, behaviors, and attitudes:

- Understanding and respecting the rights of others

- Accepting that others do not exist to serve you, and reducing or eliminating any tendency toward exploitation and manipulation

- Not expecting that others are the same as you in terms of values, attitudes, beliefs, and so on; reacting to them as separate and different than you

- Reducing or eliminating your emotional susceptibility so that you do not become enmeshed or overwhelmed by others' projections and/or emotions

- Repelling external assaults (such as projections) and not incorporating them into your self and acting on them

- Protecting yourself and respecting others

These are very important outcomes, and are combined with the most important benefit that boundary strength can offer: preventing you from being narcissistically wounded. With sufficient boundary strength, cutting, criticizing, and blaming comments do not get to your self and inflict wounds. You are less likely to have your guilt and shame triggered, you rely more on your self-perception and values, and you do not take responsibility for others' thoughts and feelings.

It takes time and effort to build your boundary strength, and it will not happen overnight. So, be patient with yourself, and resolve to stick with the program. This program begins with a self-assessment in which you try to pinpoint what, how, and when your boundaries are breached. For example, are there particular times, events, or people that seem to easily overwhelm you with emotions, demands, or expectations? When you encounter these situations or people, do you end up doing things you don't want to do? Could it be that you are so open to others that you become easily enmeshed and act more in accord with the other person's feelings than your own? This self-reflection can be valuable to help you determine the steps you can take.

The next step could be to reduce your emotional susceptibility so that you don't have to have rigid boundaries, where no one can get to you; soft boundaries, where almost everyone can get to you; or spongy boundaries, where others can unexpectedly get to you. You can reduce this susceptibility in a number of ways, and you must find what works best for you. In the short term, these are some nonverbal strategies that can help:

- Don't orient your body toward the other person. Stand or sit so that you are somewhat turned away from him.

- Don't maintain eye contact. Look at the person's forehead, just past his ears, or even across the room.

- Bring another person into the conversation.

- Change the topic when you sense that your emotions are intensifying or that the other person is trying to manipulate you.

- Keep a physical barrier of some sort between you and the other person. Anything can serve as a barrier—pillows, a purse, a book, or any medium-sized object.

- Leave, move away, or take a break (for instance, going to the bathroom) when you begin to feel the slightest discomfort.

Other behaviors such as these can do much to reduce the incidences when your emotional susceptibility leads you to become overwhelmed or enmeshed.

Once you can do some of these things to reduce your emotional susceptibility, you can begin to also concentrate on strengthening your understanding of yourself as separate and distinct from others. That's where the true boundary strength is, and your nonconscious and unconscious understanding of this is where the real work is done. Because this work is done below your conscious state, it can be difficult. But it is not impossible, as people can and do grow and develop throughout their lives.

Become Your Own Person

You may be asking what it means to become your own person and how can this be accomplished. Becoming your own person means that you do all of the following:

- Examine your values and choose them.

- Act in accord with your ethics and morals.

- Accept and respect yourself and do the same for others.

- Respect the rights of others.

- Gain the ability to connect with others in meaningful ways.

- Carefully consider others' needs and desires but resist being controlled, manipulated, or confined by these.

- Acknowledge that you are creative and always growing and changing.

EXAMINE YOUR VALUES AND CHOOSE THE BEST FIT

This examination is intended to help you find or develop the values that work best and are truest to you today. The process can also help you determine if you are continuing to act on values you unconsciously incorporated and/or values that were taught or imposed in earlier times but that don't fit who you want to be now. You can now make a conscious effort to discard things that no longer work for you or are at odds with the person you think you are or the person you want to become. You can make a conscious choice to select new values that have been examined and are freely chosen.

During your examination period, you can also reflect on your actions and measure these against your values. Failure to live up to your values can produce guilt, and acting in accord with your values is one way to reduce or eliminate some guilt feelings. Examples of some values include the following. You can value:

- A purposeful and meaningful life

- Committed relationships

- Keeping promises

- Fairness and equitable treatment and opportunities

- Getting and giving support and encouragement

- Open and honest discourse

- Civility, courtesy, and sensitivity to others

- Respect for yourself and others as worthwhile, unique individuals

- Tolerance for differences

- Care and concern for loved ones

- Kindness and positive regard for all

ACT IN ACCORD WITH YOUR ETHICS AND MORALS

When your actions reflect your values, this will keep you on the right track and permit you to lessen opportunities for feeling shamed. Your actions speak louder than your words, and you want your actions to be consistent with what you believe.

You may want to take some time to reflect on just what ethical principles and moral beliefs you have. Ethics are principles of right and wrong, and morals are judgments about the goodness or badness of actions and character.

RESPECT YOURSELF AND OTHERS

Respecting yourself and others sounds so simple, but in reality it's very complex. Respect includes an awareness of self and others as being separate, distinct, unique, and worthy. Physical and psychological boundaries are recognized, and actions convey this recognition and acceptance. It could be helpful to remember that someone with a Destructive Narcissistic Pattern (DNP), those who are self-absorbed but not quite to the level of a DNP, and others who have some aspects of undeveloped narcissism cannot recognize and accept their boundaries and those of others. They violate these boundaries because they fail to recognize them, think that they are entitled to do so, dismiss them as unimportant, do not care, or have failed to develop a sense of where they end and where others begin. Some indicators of respecting yourself include the following:

- Refusing to be manipulated into doing things you do not want to do or that aren't in your best interests

- Saying no and sticking to it

- Abiding by your ethics and morals

- Acting in accordance with your values

- Appreciating yourself, flaws and all

- Considering your needs, wishes, and desires

- Having a set of standards to guide your conduct

Some signs of respect for others include the following:

- Behaving with civility and courtesy

- Asking for permission before entering their personal space, using their possessions, and so on

- Accepting differences, such as opinions, values, and the like

- Taking what the person says and does seriously

- Recognizing their positive characteristics

One word of caution: Don't expect that you are entitled to get your way just because you express your opinion or preference and the other person listens to and accepts it. Listening and accepting is respect, and that is all you can expect.

CONNECT WITH OTHERS IN MEANINGFUL WAYS

Meaningful connections will enrich your life. This is worthwhile in all your relationships—family, friends, other social relationships, work, and so on. Some of the elements of a meaningful relationship are as follows:

- Mutual respect and acceptance

- Respect for each other's psychological boundaries

- Empathy

- Trust

- Openness and directness when expressing emotions, wants, needs, and desires

- Sensitivity to each other's moods, needs, and so on

- Giving and receiving support and encouragement

- Concern for each other's welfare and well-being

- Dependability and responsibility

Relationships provide a feeling of personal attachment, social integration, being nurtured, and reassurance that you are valued and worthy. Your meaningful relationships reduce or eliminate loneliness and isolation, help you cope with stress, and protect your health, and are related to resilience, hardiness, and optimism. The positives are many and strong.

RESPECT OTHERS' RIGHTS

The other people you encounter and relate to impact and influence you. It can be helpful to your relationships to carefully consider others' desires and needs and avoid focusing primarily (or entirely) on your desires and needs. However, you also do not want to give others' desires and needs so much importance that yours are ignored or neglected, attending to others to the extent that you become controlled, manipulated, or confined. There is a balance that must be found and maintained.

Central to finding and maintaining this balance is identifying and relinquishing your faulty beliefs about what you should do and be. Some faulty beliefs that may be affecting you are the following:

- I should be perfect.

- I should never make mistakes.

- I am responsible for how others feel.

- Others must treat me fairly.

- It's my fault if I am rejected.

- I'm to blame if things don't go my way or as I planned them.

- If I love someone, he must love me in return.

- Everyone must like and approve of me in order for me to feel adequate.

DEVELOP CREATIVITY AND GROW

Don't allow yourself to be static, complacent, and stuck in your ways, refusing to change and grow. You are never too old to learn something new, to continue to be creative in many ways, or to grow and change. It's not so much that you're searching for something, but rather you are enhancing the self that you have developed and love.

Build your creativity by looking at your world with the intent of seeing something that you didn't see before. Seek new ways of expressing yourself through your works and everyday life. Trying new processes, developing new and novel things, and even thinking in new ways are all parts of creativity. If you are so inclined, you may want to sample the creative and performing arts, to experience what they are like and what they release or develop within you. You have to seek these out; they don't look for you. But what you may find is that you are enriched and enhanced by participation.

Become Your Own Person

Specific suggestions include the following:

- Don't expect others to fix you, rescue you, or make you happy.

- Cultivate hope, optimism, and altruism.

- Don't obsess about that which you cannot control or change.

- Learn something new frequently.

- Be patient and accepting of yourself.

- Visualize the person you want to be.

To become your own person requires considerable self-examination and a careful choice of your beliefs, attitudes, and values. You examine those you currently possess, judge their usefulness for your life, and think about how these define you as a person. This examination allows you to reject those you have incorporated and acted on without conscious thought, to keep those you think fit you, and to develop others you want to have but did not consciously understand that you lacked.

You don't behave in ways that fail to show respect for the uniqueness and value of yourself, and you extend this respect and acceptance to others. You are accepting and comfortable with individual differences, and you also allow yourself to be as you are without demanding that everyone be like you or that you must be like others. Differences in others are not perceived as threats to who you are.

Other positive outcomes can include the following:

- You become less dependent on others' approval and lessen your need for external validation.

- You control and manage your anxiety better so that you do not act in ways that tend to intensify the anxiety or that are contrary to your values and ethics.

- You value the input of others, but you act in accord with your inner self.

- You have freedom to become more creative and understanding of yourself and of others, and you promote being centered and grounded

Given all these positives, becoming your own person is a worthwhile endeavor. Some of the work you can do yourself, through self-reflection and self-exploration; some of the work can be done when completing the exercises in this book; and some may need the guidance and expertise of a mental health professional. The latter can be especially helpful when exploring family-of-origin factors. You will be pleased at what happens for you when you put forth the effort to become your own person and give up beliefs, perceptions, attitudes, values, and so on that you unquestioningly accepted and acted in accord with, but that did not fit with who you wanted to be. You are now determining the person you want to be and acting to make it happen. The modest changes proposed in this chapter are a start. They are doable and can help you begin to formulate your own set of shifts.

Exercise 8.3: Your Small Shifts

Materials: One to two sheets of paper, a 12-inch ruler, and a pen or pencil for writing

Procedure:

1. Use the ruler to draw five columns on the paper. Make the first two columns 2½ inches wide, and use the remainder of the paper for the other three columns.

2. Title the columns in this order:

Column 1: "Area"

Column 2: "Shifts I Can Make"

Column 3 to 5: "Checkup," "Checkup 2," and "Checkup 3"

3. Write the following in column 1 (Area), leaving vertical space between them:

   a. "Build awareness"

   b. "Reduce self-absorption"

   c. "Cultivate my strengths"

   d. "Recognize my boundaries"

   e. "Become my own person"

4. In column 2, list the behavior and attitude changes you can make that will be a shift for you in each of these areas. Try to avoid listing major goals and objectives at this point. You may know where you want to go with changes, but limit yourself at this point to very small and modest changes.

5. In column 3, put a date by each change you listed in column 2. This is your first checkup date. While it may be tempting to use the same date for all shifts, just stop and think. Even if you only list two changes in each area, this adds up to ten shifts. That may be expecting too much at one time. However, if it seems reasonable to you to do so, then make that choice.

6. Repeat step 5 for columns 4 and 5, setting dates for a second and third checkup for each shift.

You now have your personal action plan with review dates. You can evaluate your progress at these times, celebrate your successes, formulate new small shifts, and revise and proposed shifts that were not as successful as you wished. If you persist with making small and modest changes, you will realize your more overarching goals and be much further along in building your self.

CHAPTER 9

Get to the Ideal: Build a New and Better Self

Let's take a look at the person you want to be so that you have an opportunity to determine if your ideal self is realistic and achievable, or if you have unrealistic and unobtainable goals for your self. You will want to have goals that have a good probability of attainment so that you increase your satisfaction with your self, thereby increasing your self-esteem, self-confidence, and self-efficacy. Examining your current self versus your ideal can also identify where you need to make changes and where you've already made changes that bring you closer to your desired goal, and suggest some specific strategies that may be helpful. Following is a short scale that can get you started. There are only three items for each category, but there are numerous others that could be included for each, and you are encouraged to add other items that seem relevant for you.

The Realistic and Also Ideal Self Scale

For ease of discussion, let's divide the self into the following categories:

Physical—perceptions, attitudes, and behaviors related to the body

Emotional—feelings experienced or suppressed, self-control

Relational—connections to other people

Cognitive—related to mental states, thinking, and the like

Creative—the search for new ways of seeing, doing, and
awareness

Inspirational—transcending to connect with the universe

Directions: First, rate your current level of satisfaction with each of the following, and then rate what you want or would like to be (your ideal) for the item.

5—Extremely satisfied

4—Very satisfied

3—Somewhat satisfied

2—A little satisfied

1—Not at all satisfied

Physical	Current	Ideal
1. A healthy diet	5 4 3 2 1	5 4 3 2 1
2. Regular exercise	5 4 3 2 1	5 4 3 2 1
3. Lack of drug or alcohol use or overuse	5 4 3 2 1	5 4 3 2 1
Emotional		
4. Feeling a wide and varied range of emotions	5 4 3 2 1	5 4 3 2 1
5. Expressing a variety of emotions	5 4 3 2 1	5 4 3 2 1
6. Managing and contain difficult emotions	5 4 3 2 1	5 4 3 2 1

Relational

7. Degree of intimacy	5 4 3 2 1	5 4 3 2 1
8. Conflict resolution (not avoidance)	5 4 3 2 1	5 4 3 2 1
9. Psychological boundary strength	5 4 3 2 1	5 4 3 2 1

Cognitive

10. Clear thought patterns	5 4 3 2 1	5 4 3 2 1
11. Problem-solving skills	5 4 3 2 1	5 4 3 2 1
12. Decision-making skills	5 4 3 2 1	5 4 3 2 1

Creativity

13. Imaginative	5 4 3 2 1	5 4 3 2 1
14. Open to new ideas, processes	5 4 3 2 1	5 4 3 2 1
15. Creative endeavors	5 4 3 2 1	5 4 3 2 1

Inspirational

16. Appreciating beauty, wonder, joy	5 4 3 2 1	5 4 3 2 1
17. Meaning and purpose in life	5 4 3 2 1	5 4 3 2 1
18. Zest for life and living	5 4 3 2 1	5 4 3 2 1

Scoring

There are three sets of scores that can provide information: an average score for each category for current and for ideal; total scores for current and ideal for each category; and a discrepancy score between current and ideal for each item or category. All are easy to compute, and as noted in the scoring steps that follow, each gives you a different piece of information.

1. To calculate average scores, add your ratings for the three items in a category and divide than number by three. For example, if your ratings for Current Physical were 3, 2, and 5, the average would be 3.3. Calculate averages for Current for each category first, then calculate the averages for Ideal for each category. Enter these numbers in the grid.

2. To calculate total scores, add the ratings for the items in a category, first for Current, and then for Ideal. Using the previous example, suppose your Ideal ratings for physical were 4, 4, and 5, the total would be 13. Enter these numbers in the grid.

3. To calculate discrepancy scores, subtract the lesser score from the higher score for the average rating and total scores for each category and enter these in the grid. For example, suppose your average for Current Inspirational was 3.6 and was 4.2 ofr Ideal. The discrepancy would be .6.

The higher average and total current scores indicate that you have a greater level of satisfaction in those categories. The lower discrepancy scores indicate a closer relationship between current and ideal, where you are achieving or almost achieving your ideal self for that category.

The categories with the lowest satisfaction ratings can be the areas where you need to do the most work and make the most changes, and these can be the basis for your planned actions. You may want to include any areas where the current rating is lower than the ideal for targeted change. The items for each category are some suggested areas where you could make changes. For example, if your problem-solving skills are not up to your ideal level, this is an area where you could work to improve.

You may find it helpful to develop an action plan to guide you, to be a reminder for what you want to become, and to be a mechanism for assessing your progress. Try the following exercise to help you develop your action plan.

Grid

	Physical	Emotional	Relational	Cognitive	Creative	Inspirational
Average Current Score						
Total Current Score						
Average Ideal Score						
Total Ideal Score						
Discrepancy (Average Current-Ideal)						
Discrepancy (Total Current-Ideal)						

Exercise 9.1: Your Real to Ideal

Materials: Six 5 by 8-inch index cards and a pen or pencil for writing

Procedure:

1. Write the name of one category at the top of each card, so that each category has a separate card.

2. Do the following for each card:

    a. Review the items on the scale for that category and your ratings. If you can, try to think of additional items.

    b. Write one or more desired goals that would give you the highest ideal rating for the category. In other words, in that category, what goals, if met, would get you the closest to your ideal?

    c. List any barriers or constraints that prevent or interfere with achieving your goal.

    d. Review your goals and your barriers and constraints and assess their realistic potentials. If the goal is not realistic, don't discard it yet, but do write a more realistic goal.

    e. Now, write two or three objectives for each goal. These are small changes or steps that you can take to reach your goal. Also assess these for realism.

    f. Develop a short list of strategies, behaviors, and the like that you can implement to meet each of your objectives. Don't list too many of these, but try to have two or three for each objective.

    g. Finally, review what you wrote. Make a new list of three actions you intend to take or implement, and give each a priority number (1 = first priority, 2 = second, and so on). This will be your action plan for that category. When you accomplish these actions, go back and select some others to implement.

3. Review your cards periodically and judge the extent to which you have changed in the desired direction. Revise goals and objectives that turn out to be unrealistic or unattainable. Celebrate even small successes and changes. These will encourage you.

BECOMING YOUR IDEAL SELF

Chapter 7 presented some strategies to strengthen your self that included the following:

- Building meaning and a purpose for your life that reflects your choices, values, and principles

- Reducing or eliminating isolation, alienation, and self-absorbed behaviors and attitudes that may be negatively affecting your relationships

- Becoming more centered and grounded so that choices and decisions are yours and are not unduly influenced by what others think you should be and do

Chapter 8 continued this growing and developing process with some guidance on how you can determine the person you want to be. We are all continually in the never-ending process of developing our selves, and it is through this work and effort that we become the person we want to be. In order to understand the many and varied facets of self that contribute to the whole person, chapter 8 addressed the following:

- Building awareness so that you are more fully in the moment, understand what you are doing and experiencing and why, and becoming more sensitive to the impact of your behavior and attitudes on others

- Increasing self-reflective thoughts and ideas to deepen self-understanding

- Identifying and cultivating your strengths and not becoming fixated on perceived weaknesses

- Developing strong and resilient psychological boundaries so that you choose what you take in and react to and are not either catching others' emotions or cut off from others

- Actively choosing your values and principles based on your perceptions, values, and principles that may or may not include those of your parents or other influential people in your life

- Learning to act in accord with your ethics and morals as a means to reduce guilt and shame and to live more fully

This chapter continues that process for developing your self with suggestions for how to increase and strengthen that self. These suggestions include:

- Empathic attunement and responding

- Creative thoughts, actions, and ideas

- Inspiration to connect to the universe and to develop a sense of belonging

- Cultivating and strengthening relationships

- Building your ability and capacity to let go of grudges and resentments (discussed in chapter 10)

Empathic Attunement and Responding

Do you confuse empathy and sympathy? Many people do because they don't really understand what empathy is. Empathy occurs when you sense and feel the emotions of the other person without losing the sense of yourself as a separate and distinct person. Thus, you do not get caught up in, enmeshed with, or overwhelmed by another person's feelings. You may sense what the other person feels, but you are able to both feel that and retain a sense of being separate. People with poor or inadequate boundary strength can feel the other person's feelings, but they do not retain their sense of being separate. This is what happens when you catch others' feelings, such as what can occur in interactions with your self-absorbed parent. Catching others' feelings is why some people think that they have too much empathy; they are overly sensitive to others' feelings and as a result can feel taken over, manipulated, conned, and so on. Sufficient boundary strength permits you to be empathic without experiencing the negative effects.

Until you build sufficient boundary strength, you may need to be able to sense what the other person may be feeling and respond on that basis, without entering the person's experience and feeling what she is feeling. This would allow you to make empathic responses without the danger of becoming enmeshed or overwhelmed. A vital component in being empathic is to feel what the other person is feeling, and that component is what ensnares you so that you get lost in that other person's experience, take on their feelings, make them part of you, and find that it is difficult or impossible to shake these acquired feelings. You don't want this to happen to you, but neither do you want to cut yourself off from others' feelings to the point where you don't know or understand what they are feeling.

A first step in beginning to make empathic responses is to practice identifying the feelings expressed by another person who is not expressing these directly. Many times people think they are directly expressing feelings, but they are really expressing thoughts or are expressing feelings indirectly. Try to identify the feelings of the speaker in the following statements:

"You're wonderful!"

"I'm uncomfortable."

"It's a beautiful day."

"I don't like this."

"Why are you doing that?"

If you know the speaker well, you may be able to accurately guess what she is feeling. On the other hand, even if you do think you know the person, you are just as likely to be wrong in your guess as to be right. The person may think she is direct, but the feelings are concealed and indirect. Further, there could be several possible feelings for each statement. So, it's not easy to identify the feelings. For the sake of discussion, let's suppose that the following feelings in italics are the ones the person is experiencing:

"You're wonderful."—I'm very *pleased* with what you did.

"I'm uncomfortable."—I'm *anxious and jittery*.

"It's a beautiful day."—I'm *happy*.

"Why are you doing that?"—What you are doing is very *irritating* to me.

The next steps would be for you to respond by speaking the feeling the speaker is communicating verbally or nonverbally (reflection) first and then adding what you want to say. For example, the exchange for the first two statements may go like this:

"You're wonderful!" Response: "You are pleased with what I did, and I enjoyed doing that."

"I'm uncomfortable." Response: "You seem anxious and jittery. What seems to be causing this reaction?"

Notice that you first respond by letting the person know that you understand what she may be feeling before you give your input. You accomplish two things when you do this: you let the person know you heard and understood her, and you perform a validity check to determine if you are accurate in hearing and understanding the content and the feelings in the message. All this seems pretty simple and easy, but it can be difficult to change how you customarily respond.

Exercise 9.2: A Challenge

1. For one day, pay attention to how often you respond without first reflecting the direct or indirect feelings back to the speaker.

2. The next day, practice reflecting feelings first, and note how your conversations flow. This is especially effective with children.

Practice identifying feelings and giving a reflecting response and you will find that you become better at making empathic responses. When you feel your boundaries are sufficiently strong and resilient, you can begin to open yourself so that you really feel what the other person is feeling without losing yourself in her emotions or losing the sense of yourself as separate and distinct from her. That is, you can be empathic. Until you can reach this point, you will be better served in interactions with your self-absorbed parent by limiting your responses to a more distant, reflective style.

Before ending this section, let's practice some empathic responses when your self-absorbed parent says things designed to demean, devalue, or upset you. You don't have to take offense, let this get to you and inflict pain, fight back, agree with the put-downs, or even be empathic. Then why even bother giving a reflective response? Well, such a response can help keep the focus on the other person, and that protects you from catching her feeling or projection acknowledges her feelings and intent, but does not commit you to agree or disagree.

Self-Absorbed Parent	Your Reflective Response
You don't ever seem to be able to get it right.	You're unhappy with what I did. It bothers you when things aren't done right.
Brian is so much more intelligent (handsome, talented, and so on).	You really admire Brian.

You look silly (doing, wearing) that.	You don't like what I'm (doing, wearing).
Why on earth would you do something dumb like that?	You're annoyed that I didn't live up to your expectation for me.
You're so (inept, dumb, and so on).	It irritates you that I make mistakes.
No matter how hard you try, you will never get any better.	You're disappointed in my progress.

The example for each statement represents only one of many reflective responses you can make. When you use responses such as these, you will discover that they give you time to think instead of immediately having your negative feelings triggered. Reflective responses put the focus on the other person and her feelings, and these responses allow the other person to clarify what she meant if your reflected response identified the wrong feeling. For example, in the first statement the person may have really meant that she is annoyed with herself for not doing whatever it was. That would mean that you don't have to incorporate her opinion about you. It's really about her.

Creativity

Creativity appears in many forms, and your first task is to become more open and aware of your potential for creativity, your creative endeavors, and the wide range of possibilities that are available for you to explore which will enhance and expand your creativity. Try to not think of creativity as being associated only with talent, as that will limit you too much. If you are linking the two, then you can think that only some people can be creative, that you can be creative in only one or two ways, or that you must have an inborn ability or capacity. When you look at people who receive recognition for their talents and creativity, they do seem to fit the last description. However, the definition and description we will use are the hallmarks of healthy adult narcissism, are available to everyone, can be developed, and are not dependent on native talent. Anyone can practice this form of creativity.

Creativity, as used here, includes the following:

- Developing new ways to do things and solve problems

- Perceiving things from a new perspective

- Bringing a fresh, new, or novel approach to something that already exists

- Engaging in creating something that brings you pleasure

- Learning something you did not know and making constructive use of the knowledge

- Streamlining, correcting, reducing, or eliminating barriers, constraints, and roadblocks

- Trying something different

There is a popular saying about thinking outside the box. That is the essence of creativity—to think in new and different ways, from other perspectives, and to be open to trying what has not been tried before. But you begin by cultivating a willingness to reach out for new ideas, thoughts, and so on.

Let's try an exercise to stimulate your creative thoughts.

Exercise: 9.3: Creative Thoughts

Materials: An out-of-date magazine, paper, and a pen or pencil for writing

Procedure: Look at the magazine, or if you don't have one, imagine that one is available.

1. List all the things that could be done with the magazine. Give yourself a number to try for, such as twenty things. Here are some to get you started:

   - Lining a bird cage

   - Cutting out pictures and framing them

   - Creating an altered book

   - Rolling the magazine up, tying it with cord, and using it as a log

   - Putting it under the leg of a table to keep it steady

2. Once you have completed your list, do one of the items on your list using the magazine.

Pay attention to how you felt during the exercise and how you feel after carrying out one of your ideas. You can increase your enjoyment, pleasure, and delight through your creativity. However, not all the benefits of increasing your creativity will be strictly personal. Thinking creatively can also do the following:

- Show caring and concern for family (for instance, when you make them new meals)

- Beautify the environment inside your home and outside, in your yard

- Save money by fixing the stuff that breaks or doesn't function well

- Bring beauty into your life and that of others

- Demonstrate problem solving in a way that teaches others how to do it

- Encourage and support others' creativity

- Inspire others with a feeling of excitement and curiosity

- Model openness, acceptance of challenges, and the ability to change

When you are creative, you are not locked inside yourself, are more available to others, and have a zest and excitement in your life. These are all very positive outcomes of developing your creativity.

Each person will have an individual way to unleash her creativity, and your challenge will be to find your own unique method. You may have to try a lot of things before you find those that suit you, but don't become discouraged. Keep trying and you'll find it. To get started, you can do one or more of the following:

- Recall what you did that gave you pleasure as a child that could be a creative endeavor today, and pursue it.

- Take a class in something that interests you that will lead to creative products and thoughts.

- Use the procedure in the exercise on creative thoughts for other items, procedures, and processes.

- Buy a kit from a craft store and complete it.

- Pull out your cookbook, look in a magazine, or go online and try some new recipes.

- Sketch your surroundings.

- Write a poem, story, or essay.

- Find a new use for something you intend to throw away.

You are the best person to decide what would be creative for you. Just go ahead and do it.

Inspiration

Spirituality or inspiration has been found to be of physical, emotional, and psychological benefit. It encompasses religion but is more extensive than religion per se. In fact, you don't have to be religious to be spiritual. Since there are many who will reject the notion of spirituality, fearing that it really means religion, I've elected to use the term "inspiration" to define the space between existing and acting where you transcend yourself and become connected to the universe. Inspiration is the uplifting, encouraging, sustaining, and joyous realm where you can feel less isolated and alienated, even when alone, because of the deep connectedness to the universe you feel to be a part of your life.

Why cultivate inspiration? How can this make a difference in giving up grudges, resentments, and the like? How does inspiration do anything to prevent or moderate narcissistic wounding? Inspiration works in indirect ways, as do so many other aspects of your life. It helps you be optimistic, hopeful, resilient, less prone to beating up on yourself, and better able to accept yourself as you are and others as they are. You become better able to let go of the small stuff, to recognize what is relevant and what is not, and to stay focused on the important things in your life.

Earlier in the book, I identified feelings of helplessness and hopelessness as part of narcissistic wounding. The guilt and shame that can be aroused is a part of what keeps these wounds from healing, as are the hidden thoughts and beliefs that you are not good enough or that you will never overcome the deficit. Sometimes, no amount of external support and approval, self-talk, or even success are sufficient to mediate these negative effects on the self. We have all read about extremely successful people who are admired and get positive attention but who continue to do self-destructive things or who write that they never feel that they are good enough. Instances like these illustrate how devastating and persistent narcissistic wounding can be.

You've probably made some progress on healing your wounds and in developing and fortifying your self to prevent, eliminate, and reduce this wounding. Keep working and you will get better. Adding inspiration is another positive step that will pay dividends of positive outcomes. Try the following exercise to get started or to reexperience your inspirational side.

Exercise: 9.4: Your Inspirational Side

Materials: A sheet of paper; a set of crayons, felt markers, or colored pencils; and a pen or pencil for writing

Procedure: Find a place to sit and work where you will not be disturbed.

1. As you sit in silence, close your eyes and imagine one of the following scenes with you in it:

    a. A situation where you felt cared for and cherished

    b. A time when you felt connected to the universe

    c. Your favorite place in your home that brings feelings of pleasure and contentment

    d. A situation that produced joy for you

2. Once you have the scene and images, open your eyes and draw the scene.

3. When your drawing is complete, look at it carefully and pay attention to the feelings it evokes in you.

4. Make a list of these feelings. The images and feelings are part of your inspirational life.

There are many ways to get in touch with your inspirational life and to help grow and expand it. Sometimes you even access it through other parts of your life, such as the creative process, your work, and your service to others. However you get to it, you will find that it now enriches your spirit, helps with meaning and purpose, inoculates and sustains you during adversity, and increases your awareness and enjoyment of your life. Other ways to get in touch with your inspirational life include the following. Select those that best fit you, trying one or more that are new to you. Then pay attention to what emerges. None will work immediately, but any can work over time.

- Meditation

- Religion and prayer

- Creative endeavors

- Reading inspirational books

- Writing your expressive thoughts

- Centering and grounding ceremonies

Cultivating Relationships

The first step in cultivating and strengthening your relationships is to review their quality and your current satisfaction with them. The following scale lists the core characteristics of meaningful, satisfying, and enduring relationships.

Relationships Scale

Since you have many and varied relationships, I'll ask you to rate your satisfaction with various characteristics of relationships for six categories of relationships, as follows:

Intimate adult—spouses, lovers, partners (IA)

Created family (current)—your children, grandchildren, in-laws (CA)

Family of origin—parents or parent figures, siblings, aunts, uncles, grandparents, cousins (FO)

Friends—your definition, both current and past (FR)

Work—colleagues, supervisors, bosses, staff (WO)

Social and recreational—casual acquaintances (SR)

Ratings

5—Extremely satisfied

4—Very satisfied

3—Somewhat satisfied

2—Somewhat dissatisfied

1—Not at all satisfied

Characteristic	IA	CF	FO	FR	WO	SR
1. Mutual respect, acceptance, and positive regard	—	—	—	—	—	—
2. Empathy	—	—	—	—	—	—
3. Fun playfulness	—	—	—	—	—	—
4. Responsibility	—	—	—	—	—	—
5. Trust	—	—	—	—	—	—
6. Emotional expression	—	—	—	—	—	—

Scoring: Review your ratings and determine which relationships are most satisfying, which need attention, and which are not satisfying. Next, look at the characteristics that are least satisfying for each category of relationship. These can be clues for needed changes so as to become more satisfying, or they can signal that the relationship is not a constructive one for you. You will want to have relationships that have these characteristics, where you are both giving and receiving these.

MUTUAL RESPECT AND ACCEPTANCE

Respect for each other as unique, worthwhile, and valued individuals is basic for a loving relationship. You want to feel cherished, as if you matter, that you are significant and important in the other person's life, and you give the same in return. Acceptance, like respect, is focused on the person as she is, not as you want her to be, or only if she were to change. Acceptance as you are does not mean you cannot or should not change some behaviors. For example, if neatness is important to the other person and you tend to not be neat, you may want to try to be neater as long as the demand for neatness is not excessive.

EMPATHY

Empathy is a wonderful experience where the person feels fully understood. It is also a rare experience. Some people equate empathy with sympathy, or with becoming overwhelmed or enmeshed in someone's feelings, but these states are not what empathy is about. These are cognitive responses in the case of sympathy, and lack of boundary strength for the other two. As discussed, empathy occurs when you can sense the inner experiencing of the other person and can tune in to what is being felt *without* losing your sense of yourself as being separate and distinct from her. You are not left with residual feelings that you are unable to let go of, as happens when you become overwhelmed or enmeshed.

That said, empathy is very important for a meaningful, satisfying, and loving relationship, and it should be reciprocal. You must both give and receive empathy; it shouldn't be one-sided. It is not necessary to always be empathic, but it's important to feel it frequently.

Do not confuse empathy with agreement. Just because someone understands what you are feeling, it doesn't mean that she agrees with your feelings or the rationale behind them. For example, suppose you are angry and hurt at a remark made by a friend. Your lover can empathize with your anger and hurt but still retain enough separation and individuation to disagree that the remark was insensitive, acknowledging only that it appeared that way to you. Countless fights and disagreements have resulted from an expectation that empathy means agreement. When agreement was not forthcoming, the person became angry, feeling that if her partner really loved her and understood how she felt, then the person would agree with her. This is not how empathy works.

FUN AND RESPONSIBILITY

An element of fun and playfulness enlivens any meaningful relationship. But, unless that is counterbalanced with responsibility on the part of both parties, one party is forced to assume all or most of the responsibility in the relationship. This situation can lead to developing negative feelings, where one person is focused on play and fun and the other keeps trying to get her to recognize and accept her responsibilities.

Fun and play bring out some childlike qualities, which can be endearing and can arouse one's delight and wonder. Both of you want the other to enjoy and participate in each other's version of fun and play. But, as important as this wonderful childlike spirit can be in your relationships, each person taking responsibility is equally vital.

Adult responsibilities are many, and there are times when they can appear to be overwhelming. Understandably, you probably sometimes wish that you had fewer things to be responsible for or that you could get away for a while. However, you probably just keep on trying to meet your responsibilities, even if you indulge in carping, complaining, and other acts that reveal your feelings about your plight. Think about your current lover or spouse. Does she meet her responsibilities most of the time, or, is she mostly focused on pleasure, fun, play, and the like? If the latter is the case, then fun and play is not counterbalanced with responsibility. If she tends to be overly responsible with little or no fun and play, then the other counterbalance is lacking.

TRUST

Some people end up in more than one unsuitable relationship because they inappropriately trust others. It can seem sometimes that, regardless of negative experiences such as betrayal, the person rushes back to bestowing her trust in someone rather than reflecting on her deep need to trust and working through her feelings of betrayal.

Trust is essential to the bedrock of meaningful, satisfying, and enduring relationships. When you trust the other person in a relationship, you feel that the person:

- Cares for you and has concern for your welfare

- Is open and truthful

- Understands, values, and cherishes you

- Wants the same type of relationship that you do, including the level of commitment

- Will not mislead you or push you to do things you don't want to do

- Is not out to exploit you for her advantage

Does this describe you in a relationship? You may want to take some time to reflect on your past relationships and recall some of your feelings, attitudes, and motives to see if you acted in accord with the description. If relationships in your past have failed because of betrayal of trust, then you may want to reflect on what you are seeking that allows you to overlook or ignore signs of betrayal or lack of trustworthiness. Yes, the other person acted badly, but you wanted the relationship so much that you did not take care of yourself, and it could be helpful to better understand your motives.

EMOTIONAL EXPRESSION

Trying to guess what someone is feeling can be very frustrating, even when you know the person very well. In any relationship or human interaction, there are occasions when what is felt or experienced is hidden or masked. Strong relationships are usually those where both partners are willing to be open in their emotional expressions and aware of the impact of these on the other person. Both are important for the relationship, because the other person may not be in a state or place where she can hear and understand your feelings, or is able to adequately express hers.

There are some people who do have difficulty openly expressing their feelings because of early family-of-origin experiences where open expression was not encouraged or was actively discouraged. In addition, some people have had experiences where they were ignored or hurt when they did express their feelings. Still others are unaware of experiencing mild versions of feelings, such as annoyance, and can only express very intense ones, usually in an inappropriate way. One or more of these descriptions may fit you or your partner.

If you have a relationship where your partner has difficulty expressing emotions, you can try the following:

- Instead of asking or expecting her to volunteer her feelings, give an empathic response where you identify what you sense she is feeling.

- Become more accepting and comfortable with her expression of thoughts and ideas, and don't push for expression of emotions.

- Use action words and phrases, such as "I want to hug you."

You now have a better idea of your ideal self and specific actions you can take to reach the ideal. You also have some strategies you can employ to enrich yourself and your relationships, both of which will allow you to experience a more meaningful and satisfying life. We're not quite through yet, as there are some more suggestions in the next chapter.

CHAPTER 10

You Can Do It: Taking Charge of Your Self

This final chapter presents some information and guiding exercises to help you to continue to become aware of and understand some of the forces that impacted and shaped your current self. This awareness and understanding can help you to take charge and develop the self you want to be and will suggest where and how you can change. You can also gain a better understanding of how your current reactions and relationships are impacted by your earlier relationships and experiences, and this can help you start to be more objective in your perceptions, reactions, and responses instead of just reacting and responding to the new in terms of the old.

We'll begin with a review and expansion of some topics that were introduced in previous chapters. There are exercises for you to gain more information, and some topics are new areas for self-exploration. You can find that working through these not only deepens your self-understanding, but also helps you integrate the knowledge to make changes you wish to make. After the review and expansion I'll demonstrate a process for letting go of resentment and grudges, as hanging on to these can be counterproductive for your physical, mental, and emotional well-being. This chapter provides more guidance to get you to the goal of becoming your ideal self as you defined it in chapter 9.

How you came to be was introduced in preceding chapters, and the following topics will review and expand this information. In addition, I'll make some new connections to your current experiences and suggestions for changes you may want to undertake.

- Your perceptions about your self as reflected in messages received from members of your family of origin

- How you portray the different layers or aspects of your self

- Why it is difficult to let your real self be seen, and why you maintain a facade

- Meeting others' expectations

- Acceptance and positive regard from others

- Feeling cherished and valued

THE ROLE OF EARLY EXPERIENCES IN SHAPING YOU

Your self develops over time, and its growth is influenced by an interaction of the care and nurturing experiences you received during your formative years from your family of origin, your past experiences with people other than your family of origin, and personality characteristics that are innately yours. Each person's self is different. Even some people who have the same environmental influences, such as siblings with the same parents who grew up together, are very different from each other. This is why you can differ in subtle ways from everyone else. This is one of the reasons why narcissistic wounding is uniquely individual to each person.

There is a considerable body of knowledge about the psychological growth and development of the self, and in every case, researchers and theorists emphasize the early care and nurturing received as a critical component. "Early" in this case refers to birth through the earliest formative years, birth to age six. There are some studies on prenatal influences, but these have not been tied to the psychological development of the self and are more focused on physical influences that can play a role in psychological development. We will not explore this information, as it is not directly tied to psychological development.

The basic question is "How did you come to be as you are today?" and what we'll be looking at here is some information to guide your self-exploration of your psychological development. This exploration can help you understand why you are wounded, show you a better perspective for your reactions to wounding events, and assist you to build strategies to help ward off wounding experiences. Your perception of your self is an important part of this, and your understanding of some possible early influences and experiences can be of immense help. Let's begin with some exercises to orient your thinking about possible early influences and experiences.

Exercise 10.1: Early Images

Materials: Several sheets of unlined paper; a set of crayons, felt markers, or colored pencils; and a pen or pencil for writing

Procedure: Find a place to work where you will not be disturbed and that is free of distractions. Read all the instructions before beginning the exercise.

1. Sit in silence and allow each of the following images to emerge. It could be helpful to close your eyes, but that is not essential. Consider each concept, allow the image to emerge, and then draw the image. Also list the feelings connected to each image.

    ■ Home

    ■ Mother

    ■ Father

    ■ Brothers and sisters

- Other people or relatives who were important in your early years

2. You will now have five or more images and the feelings associated with each one of these. Review your drawings and feelings, and add any additional thoughts and feelings that emerge during your review.

3. Take each image and its feelings separately and write a brief statement about your self and that image. This statement can be a feeling, another image, a memory, and so on. Just try to be as open and spontaneous as you can about images and your self.

4. Reflect on how much your current self-perception is determined or influenced by the acts and attitudes others reflect toward you.

The next exercise can be somewhat difficult in that it can be hard to maintain focus. However, you may find that your self-perception becomes clearer to you, as you will be more aware of aspects of your self that may be masked or hidden. It could also be helpful for your self-understanding to complete the exercise more than once as you begin to note changes in yourself.

Exercise 10.2: Finding Your Self

Materials: Paper, a pen or pencil for writing, and a set of crayons, felt markers, or colored pencils

Procedure: Find a place to work where you will not be disturbed, distracted, or interrupted.

1. Sit in silence and reflect on the self you present to the general public, such as colleagues at work. Think of all the characteristics they see, comment on, or even are critical or disapproving of.

Make a list of these, title it "My First Layer," and draw a picture to symbolize this layer.

2. Return to sitting in silence. Reflect on the self you present to friends and other close acquaintances. Make a list of these characteristics and try to note the difference between them and those on the previous list. For example, you may be tactful with both but are more direct with friends than with colleagues at work. These small differences can be important. Title this "My Second Layer" and draw a picture to symbolize this layer.

3. Return to sitting in silence. Reflect on the self you present to family and in other intimate relationships. Make a list of the characteristics they see. Title this "My Third Layer" and draw a picture to symbolize this layer.

4. Once again, sit in silence. Reflect on the parts of the self that you recognize but seldom, if ever, allow others to see. For example, you may have mean thoughts but would never allow anyone to know that you think that way. Make a list of these, title it "My Inner Self," and draw a picture to symbolize this layer.

5. Sit in silence, close your eyes, and allow an image of your ideal self to emerge. What does that self look and feel like? Don't try to force the image, evaluate it, or change it. Just let it come. Once you have the image, open your eyes and draw that ideal self. Title this "My Ideal Self."

6. Return to each of your lists and review what you listed and the picture you drew for each layer. You will have five drawings.

7. Place the drawings in a row and really look at them. Take note of how you feel as you review the many presentations of your self. Note how many characteristics are in the first four layers you drew that are similar and those that are different, especially when compared to your "Ideal Self."

Why Your Real Self Is Hidden

When you consider the results of exercises 10.1 and 10.2 together, you may find that you are presenting a self to others that is the result of early messages you received from others about:

- Attitudes and behaviors expected of you

- Comparisons with others made by your parents, and other important people in your world at that time about your physical attractiveness

- Comparisons with others made by your parents and other important people in your world at that time about your intelligence or abilities

- The need to maintain a facade

- Taking care of others' emotional well-being

- The extent to which you can expect to be accepted

- Your worth and value

These early messages have become so incorporated into your self that you may not even be aware of their existence until you take the time to reflect on them. They are an ingrained part of who you are but were incorporated as part of your self without conscious intent. These continue to affect your self-perception today and can play a role in determining the extent to which you become narcissistically wounded. Let's examine this list.

Expected Attitudes and Behaviors

Since you are not wounded by compliments and praise, we will focus on criticism, blame, and punishment. Do you remember being given specific directions about practice, and feedback, how you were expected to behave? Were you informed as to how your attitudes were known by others and what attitudes you were expected to have? If you are like most people, you received no instruction, direction, practice, or feedback that guided and prepared you to display expected behaviors and attitudes. You learned these primarily from the reactions of others when you did not live up to their expectations. These responses are part of the reasons you were initially wounded, and you continue to react unconsciously to anything you associate with these early responses. That leads to reinjury.

Your forming self, when you were an infant and child, was very open and vulnerable. That means that you were extremely alert and sensitive to signs of pleasure and displeasure from your primary caretaker and others around you. Everything you encountered was processed and sorted in terms of your self, and you were appropriately self-absorbed. You took in voice tone, facial expressions, how you were physically handled, and other nonverbal messages that signaled how the other person felt about you, even before you had any notion of words and their meanings. This is why you interpret some nonverbal communications you receive today in the way you do. Expected behaviors were reinforced by nonverbal signs, such as smiles and a soft and intimate voice tone. As an infant and child, you valued these positive reactions as validations of your worth and value. These were also validations of your self-perception—that is, that you were as wonderful as you thought you were.

REFLECTION: Think about how you react when you encounter an unfamiliar situation. Do you observe what others are doing and take your cues from them? Are you alert to others' reactions to you and take your cues from their positive and negative nonverbal communication? Are you wounded when you make a mistake or someone's nonverbal communication indicates disapproval? These could be some present-day associations with early learning about expected behaviors and attitudes.

Comparisons with Others

Another early experience that can contribute to narcissistic wounding is comparisons with others, especially those that portrayed you as any or all of the following:

- Inferior
- Inadequate
- Shameful
- Unlovable
- Unwanted
- Not meeting parental needs or expectations

Let's try to see if we can use a present-day example to see how the early wounding can persist and how reinjury occurs.

Exercise 10.3: Your Reactions

Materials: A sheet of paper and a pen or pencil for writing

Procedure: Sit in silence and imagine yourself in one or two of the following situations. Select the situations that have the most emotional intensity for you, and make a list of all the feelings that emerge as you recall the situation.

1. You see someone you're attracted to at a party. The person looks at you and then looks away. Their glance lingers on another person. What's your reaction?

2. A coworker doing the same tasks as you receives accolades from the boss or supervisor.

3. A person enters the main office where you work and assumes that you are not part of the workforce. You are ignored, and a stranger to the office is approached for information and directions.

4. Your mother says how wonderful one of your siblings is and how proud she is of her.

5. Your sister asks you why don't you do something that would make you more successful.

Read your reactions and note the feelings you experienced as you read the situations. Try to be honest with yourself about your hurt feelings and what the situations seemed to be saying about you. Take some time to reflect on the associations you have with remembered past events and reactions and current events and reactions.

Maintaining a Facade

When the infant's and the child's true self does not receive acceptance and approval from the mother or major caretaker, a false self emerges. If this happens continually, then the false self assumes dominance and is on display most or all of the time. It was reinforced and now is the facade that is presented to the world. It becomes more difficult for the person to access his true self, and he may have difficulty separating the two and begin to consciously accept the false self as real. That real or true self gets buried deeply and may even disappear from consciousness.

Maintaining a conscious or unconscious facade can protect the true self from wounding. After all, this true self was or is not acceptable or approved of anyway and needs all the protection it can get. Examples of a facade when wounding comments and actions are encountered include the following:

- Dismissing the wounding as unimportant

- Making sure that no one knows you are wounded

- Suppressing feelings aroused by the wounding

- Laughing it off

- Agreeing with the wounding remark or action

- Lashing out in retaliation

- Behaving with arrogance and contempt

- Pretending to be above it all

Operating under a facade does not mean that the facade is wrong or inappropriate, as there can be times and situations where it is safer for you to hide your true feelings. What can be helpful is for you to admit to yourself that you are using a facade and to stay in touch with how much you do use it. It is also helpful for you to examine yourself to see if your real self is known to you and is ever allowed to emerge. Is your real self ever allowed out? Do you even know what that real self is like? If your true self is really unknown to you and/or seldom allowed to emerge, you may be acting on early parental messages that reinforced your false self. Your challenge will be to find your true self, who you really are, and to build and reinforce it.

Taking Care of Others

It is easy to arouse your feelings of inadequacy, shame, and guilt if you are in the habit of taking care of others or believe that that is your responsibility. We're not talking about those who legitimately need taking care of here—children or those with disabilities. This is the dynamic where you feel you must take care of other adults who are presumably responsible for themselves. You can become wounded when others indicate they are uncomfortable, upset, or angry, or when they cry. Somehow you have incorporated the notion that you are supposed to prevent this from happening, and you were not good enough, or failed in your duty. Your thoughts about yourself can be something like "I must be an awful person to let this happen." You may spend a considerable amount of time and effort taking care of other people you don't even know or like just because you are acting on this long-term, firmly entrenched, old parental message that you are expected to take care of others.

Were you responsible for the physical or emotional well-being of your parent or parent figure, or even both parents? As we explored earlier in the book, this is called parentification, where the self-absorbed parent expects the child to assume responsibility for the parent's well-being, especially their emotional well-being. This is likely to have carried over to your adult life, where you unconsciously once again assume the role of caretaker.

Acceptance by Others

The need to belong and be accepted is very strong, and some think this need is a part of our DNA. There is considerable evidence that humans are social beings and that interpersonal relationships are essential to our health and sense of well-being. Thus, it is no wonder that wounding takes place when a lack of acceptance is perceived.

Some expressions of a lack of acceptance can include the following:

- A dismissive glance

- Someone curling his lip when he looks at you

- Frowns directed toward you

- Being overlooked or ignored

- Not receiving an invitation to an event

- Not receiving notification of a meeting

- No one sitting next to you at a meeting

- Being told to go away

- Laughing, jeering, or making fun of something you do or say

- Your companions going somewhere and leaving you alone

Some indicators of a lack of acceptance are nonverbal and subtle but can still have a strong impact on the receiver. And some are more direct and not subtle at all. These, too, can have a significant impact on the receiver.

The nonverbal behaviors that you perceive as a lack of acceptance are associated with some of your long-standing perceptions about your worthiness, acceptance, and lovability. These, in turn, could be related to how you were treated by your parents during your early years. Let's do an exercise to demonstrate what this means.

Exercise 10.4: Acceptance

Materials: A sheet of paper and a pen or pencil for writing

Procedure: Sit in silence and concentrate on your breathing to make it deep and even. Allow each of the following images to emerge, and write the feelings that are aroused in you for that image.

1. Your mother's expression as she looks at you. Be sure to use the first one that emerges and don't edit or change it.

2. Your father's expressions as he looks at you

3. A grandparent's or caretaker's expressions as he or she looks at you

4. A sibling's expressions as he or she looks at you

5. A teacher's expression as he or she looks at you

Review your list of feelings for each image, and try to recall a situation where you saw a similar expression on someone's face and felt accepted or unaccepted by that person. This is an example of transference.

Your Worth and Value

Some people have an inflated sense of their value and worth. They tend to be grandiose and arrogant and feel superior to other people. Some people have a deflated sense of their value and worth and feel inferior to others. Some people have both an inflated *and* deflated sense of their self that can switch places very quickly. So, in an interaction with this person, you can start out experiencing one self and tailor your responses to that, only to have the person then respond with the other. That experience can be very confusing and unsettling for the receiver. Finally, there are some people who have a realistic perception of their worth and value and do not feel superior or inferior. They can see how they are different from others, how they are unique, but they don't attach superiority or inferiority to that difference. They can feel that they and others are worthwhile and of value.

People who have an inflated perception of their worth and value, those who have a deflated perception, and those who have both perceptions can be easily wounded. The person who has a more balanced and realistic perception can also be wounded, but not easily and not often. The extent to which you are constantly and easily hurt can be a clue to your perception of how you value yourself.

Your perception of your value and worth is formed from a combination of your innate personality characteristics, your family-of-origin experiences, and your past experiences and relationships with other people. The way that other people treated and responded to you carried a powerful message about your worth and value that you incorporated into your self and identified with, and this became a part of how you see yourself. Studies abound that support the notion that how you were cared for, nurtured, and responded to are major determinants of how you perceive yourself and your sense of your value and worth. You achieve a balanced and realistic perception of your value and worth through the many experiences and relationships with others you have from the time you are born and continuing throughout your life. Thus, when you encounter a comment, action, or a situation that does not support your perception of yourself, you are wounded. The exception is the person with a deflated sense of his worth and value, who expects to be wounded and often is wounded; this wounding further confirms his deflated perception. They, too, are wounded, but that wounding is reinforcing for his already deflated self-perception.

The person with a balanced and realistic perception of his worth and value can be wounded, but this happens less often. This is because he possesses an acceptance of his personal strengths and limitations, strong and resilient psychological boundaries, an ability to get out of himself and empathize with others, and a realistic appraisal of the circumstances. This is the person who can understand that he does not have to personalize what others say or do, even when the other person's intent is to wound. If you are often wounded because others don't think you are as wonderful as you think you are (inflated self), if others see you as you see yourself and find little worth or value (deflated self), or both states alternate so that you are constantly being wounded by almost everyone, then your task and challenge is to develop a more realistic and balanced perception of your value and worth.

WHAT IS OKAY FOR OTHERS TO SEE?

Let's take a look at some of the many facets of your self and describe what you are willing to let others see.

Exercise 10.5: Facets of Your Self

Materials: Several sheets of paper, a pen or pencil, and a set of crayons, colored pencils, or felt markers

Procedures: Read all the instructions before starting to work.

1. Label four sheets of paper 1, 2, 3, and 4. These are some of the layers of your self where you allow facets of your self to be visible. You can have more than four layers if you choose. Layer 1 is public; layer 2 is for acquaintances, colleagues, and distant family; layer 3 is for intimate relationships; and layer 4 is mainly hidden from others.

2. Think about each of the following after you first read through the list. Take each one separately, focus on it, and allow an image and feeling to emerge. Don't edit or try to change the image or feeling, just let each come and be experienced.

- Your aggressive self

- Your competitive self

- Jealousy and envy

- Being wounded

- Resentment

3. As each image and feeling emerges, draw it on the sheet for the layer that best fits where you display this particular self or feeling. For example, if you keep your aggressive self hidden from almost everyone, you would put that image on the sheet numbered 4. If there are images that seem to fit on more than one layer, put them on all the layers where you think they fit.

4. After you finish, review your drawings and note the layers where you put the images.

5. Think about what emerged for the various levels and answer for yourself the following questions:

- Do you become wounded when someone seems to see a part of you that you don't want them to see?

- Are you keeping important parts of your self hidden from almost everyone?

- Are you denying, suppressing, or repressing unacceptable parts of yourself?

- Is your public face a genuine reflection of who you are and how you see yourself?

The just-completed exercise may give you some clues about personal characteristics you find shameful. Shame is experienced on many levels, such as the following:

- Embarrassment

- A desire to get away or flee

- Hoping that someone will not see a part of you that you don't like

- Feeling that you are not good enough

- Failure to live up to your own or others' standards or expectations

- Profound disappointment in yourself

- Humiliation

- A sense that you are fatally flawed and can never be fixed

A common reaction to shame is to try to cover it up. This cover-up can be to prevent others from seeing that part of you and/or to prevent you from having to experience the awfulness of shame. Cover-ups can be any of the following:

- Displacing or projecting on to another person

- Becoming angry at others or at yourself

- Blaming someone for your feelings

- Turning the tables by attacking someone else

- Crying and becoming hurt so that someone will soothe you

- Withdrawing physically or emotionally

- Trying to laugh it off

- Telling jokes

- Making sarcastic remarks

- Denigrating others

- Changing the subject if you are having a conversation

- Exaggerating your self-perceived faults

Shame is a very intense and uncomfortable feeling that manifests itself in many ways. It is also very difficult to get away from your shame, and it affects your feelings, behavior, and attitudes in unconscious ways.

The roots of your shame are located in your family of origin and their expectations for you. There may also be some cultural determinants, but the strongest influences were those early parental and family experiences that laid the foundation for what you consider to be shameful about yourself. You received parental messages about:

- The extent to which you pleased or disappointed your parents

- Their liking or dislike of you and your behavior

- Expectations for what was acceptable or unacceptable behavior

- Their comparisons of you with others

- The extent to which you measured up to their fantasy of what you "should" be

- Your ability to please them

Many of these were nonverbal and/or unconscious parental messages that were incorporated on an unconscious level, and they continue to drive what you consider shameful about you today. Some of the same old parental messages are what you hear today when you become narcissistically wounded.

You are revisiting those unconscious messages on an unconscious level, and they have not lost their power to produce shame and wounding. When you become more aware of what is happening, you can take steps to reduce the impact of these unconscious messages on you and to become the person you want to be.

This chapter has focused on how some of your family-of-origin factors contributed to shaping your current behavior and attitudes, especially those that allow you to become wounded. These are not the only factors, and they also act in very complex ways with other factors, such as past experiences and your personality.

FORGIVENESS

I'm often asked if the child of a self-absorbed parent should or has to forgive that parent, and my answer is no. Forgiveness may be possible at some point, but it is not a requirement. The child was injured at a deep level and is still being negatively impacted as an adult, and his energies are better spent on more positive pursuits, such as developing his undeveloped narcissism and establishing meaningful relationships.

The sense of relief is palpable and visible after receiving my answer, and they tell me how awful they were feeling because they could not forgive. I usually respond that they may want to forgive at some future time when they have completed enough personal work and reflection to allow forgiveness to seem possible, so that it does not carry remnants of anger and there can be a deep understanding of that parent. It's much easier to encourage forgiveness if you are an outsider and did not have to experience the daily or constant assaults on the self by the self-absorbed parent who, in many cases, is continuing these assaults. The self of the adult child has to be fortified and developed to withstand these assaults, to further grow and prosper in positive ways, and to receive internal and external validation of his meaning and worth in order to be in a place where forgiveness is possible. Don't forget that the parent probably feels and thinks all of the following (the child is referred to as "he"):

- I was right to do what I did.

- I was entitled to do what I did.

- He is wrong and shameful to question my actions, needs, and demands.

- If he was worthy, he would be appreciative of me.

- I should be admired.

- If it were not for me, he would be a mess.

- I know better what he needs than he does.

- He is too sensitive and overreacts to my constructive comments.

- Whatever I did was for his own good, and I was the best judge of that.

- He owes me everything.

It is the extremely rare person who can experience these attitudes without reexperiencing some of their childhood's negative feelings. It is also challenging and rare to be able to withstand these and to see beyond them to accurately perceive the bleakness, fear, and isolation that the parent is probably experiencing. The parent could have so much that is worthwhile but has nothing and doesn't know how to enrich his life. That has to come from within, and there are no resources there.

The deep emotional ties between parent and child can prevent the adult child from being objective and completely logical about this parent, so that the parent's negative actions, comments, responses, and the like can continue to hurt. This, too, makes forgiveness difficult, if not impossible.

It may be more helpful for the adult child to stop worrying about forgiveness but to keep it in mind as a possible option when the time is right. Try not to force yourself to forgive because others think it is the right thing to do; focus more on some interim steps that help your healing. Let's try to identify some signs that healing is progressing.

Healing is not all or nothing—it is a process that happens over time. Because it is a process, you may not be aware of its progress and you may find yourself just longing for the end result. But becoming aware that you're actually making progress can boost your spirits and help you keep working. You can use the following as a guide that healing may be progressing:

- You can reflect on your parent and accept that he is unlikely to change, and you don't strongly yearn or wish that he would change. While change is possible, you accept that you cannot force, mandate, demand, or influence the parent to change.

- Your parent's negative, demeaning, and devaluing comments don't hurt as much, and their negative impact is not as long lasting. These comments can still wound, but that wounding is decreasing.

- You may still dread interactions with your self-absorbed parent, but you don't leave from these as churned up as you did before, their effects don't last as long, and you are able to be more detached during them. You are also containing and managing your feelings better.

- You are more aware of the possibility that your reactions to your parent can get displaced on others, and you consciously work to not let this happen.

- You are better able to be empathic, and this has improved your most important relationships.

- You are more centered and grounded and have moderated your characteristic response of either being compliant or of being defiant. You are consciously trying to not relate to others as you did with your parent.

- At some level, you realize that you have the power to prevent your parent from hurting you so much and can choose to have a more measured, less hurtful response to him that does not disrespect either of you as unique and worthwhile individuals.

■ You derive satisfaction from your other relationships and give these your time, effort, and energies, receiving much in return.

■ You are able to reach out to others in your most intimate relationships to sense their feelings without becoming enmeshed or overwhelmed or wanting to get away, and you are able to connect with others in a deep and meaningful way.

When your self feels ready to forgive, that is the time to proceed. You may never fully reach this point, and that is understandable. Not being ready to forgive your parent is not shameful, nor does it need to produce guilt. You need time to heal before you can forgive.

Resentments and Grudges

An important part of building a new and better self is to let go of negative things that are sapping your energy, time, and creativity, and that are not constructive. Resentments and grudges fall into this category.

Exercise: 10.6: Old Resentments and Grudges

Materials: Several sheets of paper and a pen or pencil for writing

Procedure: Return to the lists you developed in chapter 6 (exercise 6.1). These lists were of events, people, and situations that you experienced as negative and still carried negative feelings about. If you did not complete those exercises, now is the time to do so because they will help you to focus your letting-go process. If you did complete the exercises, review your lists and note your feelings as you recall the circumstances for each. Use a separate sheet of paper for each event, person, or situation. Complete the following steps for each. List the event, person, or situation at the top of the page.

1. Note what feelings you can identify as you recall each event, person, or situation.

2. Rate the intensity of your current feelings as you do the review using a scale from 0 (no intensity) to 10 (extreme intensity).

3. Discard any events that have an intensity rating of 3 or less and put a line through it.

4. Close your eyes and try to recall images for each remaining event. Focus on the people, impressions, and so on. Pay attention to where, or if, you feel tension in your body as you do the recalling. If you do find tension, such as clenching fists or a tight chest, you may be suppressing some emotions about your experience. Note the intensity of your tension and give it a rating from 0 (no intensity) to 10 (extreme intensity). If that tension is higher than 3, put the event, person, or situation back on your list. There is a little more work to be done.

5. You should now have a list of events, people, and situations for which you carry enduring negative feelings. Some may have less intense negative feelings associated with them, and this is progress. You've come a long way and can be pleased about how much you have let go. If recalling the event doesn't hurt as much as it did before, you can be assured that you are making progress in letting go and getting over it. Notice that I've not said anything about forgiveness. You may or may not forgive those most involved in your wounding. That's up to you and is beyond the scope and purpose of this book. You can work to reduce the intensity of the negative feelings you carry without necessarily forgiving someone. You can build and fortify your self without forgiving. So, don't focus on forgiving if that is something you've tried to do. You can get and feel better just by focusing on letting go of the feelings you carry.

6. Take your list or pile of enduring feelings with ratings of 4 or higher and make a new list of these, including their intensity now. If you have some that are still rated 8, 9, or 10, you may need to work with a therapist to get better and faster results. The strategies suggested here can help reduce intensity for ratings below 8, but higher ones are deeper and have more complex roots. This is why an expert could be of more benefit.

7. You should now have a list of events, people, and situations with feeling-intensity ratings of 4 to 7. Ratings of 3 or below can indicate that these feelings are on their way out and are not troubling or of consequence to you. While this is arbitrary and dependent on your interpretations and ratings, these intensities are used as a guide and are not fixed. This new list is the one you will work to resolve.

Let's review your new list and the feelings you've noted. You've included the feelings and the intensity for each. Now, note the commonality of feelings across events, situations, and people. There is likely to be some commonality, and it may even be considerable. The next step is to identify what you think these common feelings are saying about you. The next exercise explores this.

Exercise 10.7: Your Feelings About You

Materials: The list developed from the previous exercise, a couple of sheets of paper, and a pen or pencil for writing

Procedure:

1. Note the common feelings among the items on your list or pile and make a list of these feelings. For example, you could list anger, hurt, and sadness.

2. The next step is to write next to each feeling what you think that feeling says about you. For example:

Anger—I am unable to prevent this (event, words, people, and the like) from injuring me.

Hurt—I wasn't prized, valued, or cherished.

Sadness—I fear a part of me is gone, destroyed, or does not exist.

3. Review your statements to make sure that they are focused on you and not on others. We are not able to change others, and the real feelings are most likely to be about your feelings and beliefs about yourself.

4. Next, rate how true each of the statements is about you, overall. For example, how true is it that you are unable to prevent something from injuring you? Give each a rating from 0 (not at all true) to 10 (extremely true). You will probably find that most of your ratings are at the lower end of the scale, as you now have some tools to address these statements. For example, let's suppose that you listed anger and hurt with high ratings. You could use the suggested tools whenever you have the feeling, as illustrated below.

5. Following are some feelings and associated thoughts about oneself. Each has several tools that can be used to reduce the negative feelings and thoughts about oneself.

   a. Feeling—anger (associated thought—to prevent injury to the self). Tools include strong and resilient boundaries and emotional insulation.

   b. Feeling—hurt (associated thought—not prized, cherished, and valued). Tools include self-acceptance, meaningful relationships, and blocking projections.

   c. Feeling—sadness (associated thought—loss of a part of self). Tools include developing healthy adult narcissism, creativity, and inspiration.

6. The next step is to list what resources you have and those you could develop to ease, moderate, or eliminate negative self-thoughts. Keep this list and review it on a periodic basis.

7. The final step is to return to the original list you used at the beginning of this exercise and the list of events, situations, and people from the previous exercise. Place these side by side and take each item and the feelings associated with it separately for review. Note how you now feel, especially any lessening of the intensity of negative feelings. Ask yourself if you are ready to let go of these and heal yourself. Write the feelings you think you can now relinquish on a strip of paper (or on numerous strips). Discard the strips by shredding, cutting, burning, or throwing them in the trash. Note how you feel when you are finally able to let go.

You now have a vision for changing and becoming the person you want to be, one that includes a meaningful, purposeful, and rewarding life with satisfying and enduring relationships. You can build your self to shed the inhibiting forces left over from your destructive narcissistic parent, and to help you move forward with more positive growth and development. Your deeper understanding of yourself can permit you to have more understanding, acceptance, and tolerance for others—including your parent who, unlike you, is locked in his Destructive Narcissistic Pattern without understanding or change. You can give to others what you longed for but never received from the parent, and in that giving reap considerable benefits for your self. You can protect and defend yourself and your children from the negative aspects of your destructive narcissistic parent, while at the same time enriching your life and the lives of those you hold dear. You have considerable inner resources to help you cope with adversity, make meaningful connections to others, enjoy yourself, and make positive contributions to the world.

We are now at the end of the journey that began in chapter 1, but you are only beginning your journey to heal your self, fortify your self against narcissistic injury, and let go of the unfinished business that haunts you. You are the only one who can accomplish this. You have the ability and can develop the expertise.

References

Brown, N. 1998. *The Destructive Narcissistic Pattern*. Westport, CT. Praeger Publications.

———. 2001. *Children of the Self-Absorbed*, first edition. Oakland, New Harbinger Publications.

———. 2002. *Whose Life Is It Anyway? When to Stop Taking Care of Their Feelings and Start Taking Care of Your Own*. Oakland, New Harbinger Publications.

———. 2006. *Coping with Infuriating, Mean, Critical People*. Westport, CT. Praeger Publications.

Hafen, B. Q., K. S. Karren, K. J. Frandsen, and L. Smith. 1996. *Mind/Body Health: The Effects of Attitudes, Emotions and Relationships*. San Francisco: Benjamin Cummings.

Kohut, H. 1977. *The Restoration of the Self*. New York: International Universities Press.

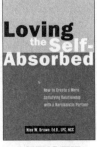
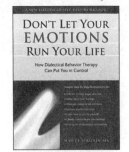